Lead by Driving Actions to Outcomes

Ask - Act – Reward

Based on the THEORY OF SELF-UTILITY with an emphasis on VOLUNTEER ORGANIZATIONS

Michel Listenberger, OD, FVI

AuthorHouse™
1663 Liberty Drive
Bloomington, IN 47403
www.authorhouse.com
Phone: 1 (800) 839-8640

Published by AuthorHouse 04/29/2015

ISBN: 978-1-5049-0960-0 (sc)
ISBN: 978-1-5049-0962-4 (e)

Library of Congress Control Number: 2015906596

Print information available on the last page.

CONTENTS

Dedicated to the memory of Dr. Phillip VanDenBerg - my mentor.

ORGANIZATIONS REFERENCED IN THIS BOOK

V.O.S.H.- International (Voluntary Optometric Services to Humanity) is the largest Non-Government Organization (N.G.O.) of Eye Care Professionals providing eye care around the world to people who cannot afford nor obtain such care. It consists of seventy-five State and National Chapters. V.O.S.H. delivers eye exams and glasses by conducting one to three week missions, supporting sustainable clinics overseas, supporting Optometric Education and local eye health education onsite. Thirty-nine million people are blind in the world and 45% are blind because they have no access to glasses.

Junior Optimist Octagon International (J.O.O.I.) is a 16,000 member Youth Organization. J.O.O.I. is under the umbrella of Optimist International and represents a "youth" membership class. J.O.O.I. is made up of Clubs in the United States, Canada and the Caribbean Nations. J.O.O.I. has an elected Youth Board of Directors and an elected Youth International President. Members experience leadership and build confidence in themselves by volunteering in their schools and communities.

Optimist International (OI) is an adult civic service organization collectively embracing "Optimism" as a positive value that enriches and propels life. Optimists provide Optimistic experiences to young people as they "Give Hope and Vision by Bringing out the Best in Kids." Optimist International is the fourth largest civic service organization in the World. Headquarters are in St. Louis and Montreal.

Niles Education Foundation (NEF) is a local (Niles, Michigan) Foundation to acquire and distribute funds in support of the Niles Community Schools for programs and projects aimed at enhancing, enriching and supplementing opportunities for students, staff and community – changing minds, changing lives.

FROM THE AUTHOR

This Book was written because someone took the first step to show an analytical introvert the real power in being a leader working with other people. By moving outside of managing my eye-care practice toward volunteer leadership roles, I quickly learned the basic process of leading which changed my life as well as the lives many others who served with me.

After a few years a system emerged from my deep interest in scientific principle being applied to changing behavior patterns in people. Philosophically a <u>Theory of Self-Utility</u> was developed which applied to everything. This Book explains how the basic "theory of <u>Self</u> driving actions to outcomes. The <u>Ask</u> initiating an <u>Act</u> resulting in a <u>Reward</u>" repeating itself in feed-back loops leads to change.

This basic system then was applied to many offices leading to mobilizing groups with positive outcomes in every attempt. My authority for writing this Book comes from this record of success leading from local to State to International Organizations.

- President of Optimist Club of Niles 1985-86 (#1 of 110 Clubs in Michigan)
- Optimist Lieutenant Governor SW Michigan (#1 of 18 zones in Michigan)

- Founding President of Michigan Voluntary Optometric Services to Humanity 1985-88 (annually conducting four annual eye care missions around the world)
- Governor of Michigan Optimists 1988-89 (#1 of 50 Internationally)
- Vice President of Optimist Region 1993-95 (#1 of 10 Internationally)
- President of VOSH-International 1995-97
- Junior Optimist Octagon International Chair and Advisor mentoring five International Youth Presidents and their Board of Directors
- President of Optimist International 2005-06 (top growth in twenty years)

The uniqueness of this Book is that it demonstrates you can change. Part One "Leadership Theory and You" shows how to change yourself and others using Ask – Act - Reward cycles to influence change. Part Two "Applied Leadership" shows ways to use the theory to lead groups and organizations. This book is primarily based in "VOLUNTEER" organizations. Instead of getting results by rewarding employees with payment of wages, this book shows how to get results by rewarding volunteers with recognition and enhancement of their self-image. Ask Act Reward is leveraged with efficiency systems from local to international.

In my life leadership was learned. You can learn to lead by practicing and embracing this basic system. Take a risk. Change your life and others around you.

FOREWORD
– ASK – ACT - REWARD

So many good books and so many good articles have been written about leadership. They talk about skills, attitudes or characteristics that make a better leader. In this book, however, we take a different approach.

Leadership is about asking people to do something; acting by doing it; and being rewarded appropriately. Leaders can use this interactive process to drive change and achieve success.

- Do this once and you change a little
- Do this often and you change a lot
- Make this your Habit and change a community
- Make this your way of life and lead the world

A good leader must understand what people emotionally want, need and fear. These can be major barriers to a person facing change, or they can be what motivate people to action. A good leader knows how to guide outcomes that turn "want and need" into passion. A good leader sees potentiality and empowers others to lead. Directing others into action multiplies outcomes.

People are a leader's greatest asset. People provide the purpose and the mission. People make the product and deliver the service.

When working together toward honorable causes a tremendous amount of self growth rewards those who interact with the leader as well as the leader himself. Personal relationships and a depth of friendships form bonds so much stronger than casual social contact. Helping others changes them and yourself in ways that give meaning to life itself.

Benefits of using this process:

- You build positive habits for yourself – and learn to break old ones
- You learn how to motivate and influence others which leads to getting results
- You proactively build more relationships acquiring "cause-based" friendships
- It's also more fun being successful

1

DEFINING LEADERSHIP

Dr Phil VanDenBerg was a tall, confident person with a great deal of patience and determination. He was not outspoken or persuasive or charismatic - he did not stand out in a crowd. His manner was mild but his intent was well formed before he even spoke. He focused on others, giving them reasons for what they didn't know they were about to do. And if after several attempts to persuade them failed, he would look gently upon them and thank them for their interest.

When asked later about how he felt after receiving rejection, he simply said the time wasn't right for them but they would come around in time - and amazingly, often they did. He also showed me that what you see of an individual is only about ten percent of the potential of their personal power and ability.

Leadership is much like an iceberg. It's not the part you see that gives a leader their power; it's what lies beneath.

DEFINITION of LEADERSHIP (Reduced to its simplest terms)

LEADERSHIP IS THE ABILITY TO CHANGE THE BEHAVIORS OF PEOPLE TOWARD A PREDETERMINED OUTCOME.

THE PROCESS OF LEADERSHIP

Leadership begins with you. It is **self driving actions to outcomes**. It is performed by mastering the science, art and habit of change.

The leadership process has its foundation in **Self**, your core being, who you are, every force that brings you into being and keeps you alive. The process of leadership comes from **Self**, **Ask**ing (driving) others, to initiate **Act**ions, that result in **Rewards** (outcomes) which returns back to **Self** (You) – changing you and others.

The leader begins with plans – a series of things to ask. What do you expect to happen? Describe the change you hope to see.

"Be the change you hope to see in the World" – *Mahatma Gandhi.*

Action is where people, groups and causes intersect and interact. It's the "flashpoint" of change. Interaction is where you make a difference.

Every interaction results in an outcome. It may be imperceptible or it may be profound! Your perceptions potentially, impact "who you are", "who others are" and "what the organization is".

Change itself occurs within a four-part "Cycle of Influence" that repeats over and over, with persistent and creative actions and interactions. If these cycles are self-directed effectively toward an outcome, great leadership blossoms!

SOME OVERALL DYNAMICS OF LEADERSHIP

Changing many people is powerful leadership. Changing toward a worthy outcome is good leadership. Winston Churchill, for example, was considered a good leader, whereas with abuse of power, Adolf Hitler was considered a bad leader.

By changing behaviors one can eventually change people, ideas and organizations. The concept starts by creating interactions with others. These interactions can change behavior and if repeated, and eventually build behavior patterns. Behavior patterns can be nourished into habits. By building and combining habits one develops a persona. People tend to believe and value what they do. These multiple behaviors can ultimately build values.

Change occurs most effectively by working within the context of a larger "group-utility" such as a social organization. It is easier to build upon a vision than to create one, it is easier to work within an organization than to build one and it is easier to modify behaviors than to create them.

Change also occurs more effectively by orienting and mentoring new leaders. It is easier to create new behaviors and leadership habits than to change old ones.

Management and Leadership

The term management is often used to denote a more technical or tracking activity. Leadership often refers to charisma and motivation. It might also be said that management is working the mission while leadership is selling the vision.

Either way, the intended purpose of outcome is the same. Realistically both mission and vision are needed to succeed. Therefore, using terms of leadership or management in our definition simply reflects a style or component of changing behavior of people. The intent is not to let perceptions clouded by terminology detract us from direct causal action plans leading to positive results. This is not to say that style or methods are not important, they are, just secondary to the primary focus - changing behavior and outcomes.

Note that there is no English term with the narrow definition of "changing behavior of people". We are not going to ignore the difference between "leadership and management" as we proceed. We will, however, consider them as different styles and approaches toward getting the same results.

Social and Emotional Considerations

Generally Self-Utility or our core inner being is most interested in pleasing itself. How do we fit in? What do others think about us? Will we be liked?

Neuroscience researchers have learned that a proportionally large amount of our cerebral cortex activity is devoted to social outcomes. But if we are truly interested in leading our self toward positive change and making a difference, we may have to put aside the more emotional aspects of social outcomes in favor of more analytical and significant long term change. Again, the overriding purpose of leadership is to change the behavior of people. And again, changing behaviors of people doesn't necessarily preclude feeling good about ourselves, it just places these feelings secondary to your larger more meaningful purpose.

As social beings it should also be understood that people often make decisions emotionally. Leaders may lead with emotion but they succeed by being accountable to outcomes. This can be seen as requiring two approaches or skill sets:

a. Charismatic leader building relationships and selling the sizzle (vision) and

b. Analytical leader managing, tracking and rewarding outcomes (mission).

Leading requires both tenants (a) to relate and sell emotionally and (b) to manage and track analytically. If you only have one of these personalities, try to partner with someone who has the other. Always remember the benefit to the greater good is the goal.

2

SELF-UTILITY AND LEADERSHIP - AN INTRODUCTION

Deep in the belly of the universe burns a fire of primordial destiny - a destiny that willed mankind into being – inspired by _The Universe is a Green Dragon_. Does the Universe itself have such a consciousness that can enable our existence? Do we even have access to a cosmic consciousness that can answer that question?

Humans are said to have the most highly developed consciousness on Earth. Can we truly connect our inner fires of self-determinism, our Self-Utility, our destiny?

While the exact nature of Self-Utility cannot be viewed as a mechanical object, its effects and outcomes can be modeled. Consider its possibilities, consider its effects and consider its reality in your life.

This book will this abstraction and focus on us, in our humanity. As a species, we are different from others in part because of our large cerebral cortex giving us the unique ability to consider cause and effect. How will our actions affect our future? The ability to ask this question, gives us, as humans, an advantage over other species, of not only capable of predicting but effecting future outcomes. Certainly our evolutions of "opposable thumbs" as well as our ability to walk upright both lead to the development of an expanded cerebral cortex. With our large cerebral cortexes, mankind has inherited dominion over the world by this ability to predict and influence outcomes. At the same time we have inherited the stewardship of being able to determine which species survive and which perish, including our own. In some ways this ability to influence the future, using good judgment and stewardship, makes humans the stewards of the world, as well as its future.

People have an inner force within them that defines their essence. This inner force empowers people toward animation, well-being and existence itself. People effect change in their lives and change in others around them by interacting with other people (relationships), ideas (vision) and organizations (collective values) around them. All of these interactions can be represented as we experience the theory's cycles.

This book is about leadership - about humans interacting. This leadership approach utilizes the principals of the Theory of Self-Utility, focusing on the idea that "People do what makes sense to them." It provides a unified perspective of a common process of operation using "Cycles of Influences" and by so doing unifies relationships with others.

The Theory of Self-Utility and its three basic Tenants are outlined. This Theory is explained in depth in the book, "SELF-UTILITY: A Theory of Everything" by Michel Listenberger, OD, FVI, Author House, 2009.

In this Book the process of leading as an aspect of Self-Utility will be explained.

SELF-UTILITY as it applies to LEADERSHIP

Your "Self-Utility", the core of your being, defines you and is expressed by all you say and do. Your "Self-Utility" initiates change through feed-back loops called "Cycles of Influence".

There are four phases of these "Cycles of Influence". The Cycle is initiated by the vital force of:

1) "Self-Utility" (your core being) creating
2) "Directives" (driving, asks). Directives, in turn lead to
3) "Actions" (behavior). Actions are the flashpoint of change – where change happens – sometimes imperceptible, sometimes profound. Actions result in
4) "Outcomes" (rewards). The Outcome then reverts back to reshaping the
       (1) Self-Utility (core being) making the Cycle complete.

Self-Utility exists and is at work in groups of all kinds. This includes families, businesses, organizations and social clubs ("Group-Utility"). To take it a step further, Self-Utility also applies to ideas, causes and movements.

For a leader to be effective in producing positive change, the Cycles of Influence must be repeated many, many times. Effective leaders must always be persistent and innovative.

Understanding the dynamics and embracing this Theory can vastly enhance your ability to be a better leader. Understanding what people need and want as well as what will mold their behavior is necessary to lead a noble mission. Both you and they will grow through interaction with these "Cycles of Influence".

Be aware that the flashpoint of change is interaction. At that point it is often measurable and observable.

"Judge a tree by the fruit it bears, not by the fruit it talks about."
– Expanded from Bible, Mathew 7:16

One way to summarize the Theory of "Self-Utility" is to say that **people do what make sense to them**. Whether you are serving as a Chief Executive Officer, on boards of directors, on committees or in organizations, make decisions that are consistent with this Theory. Ultimately, if you do this well, you can not only predict the future, you can change the future!

DEFINITIONS USED IN THIS BOOK:

A list of definitions can be found under "The Theory of Self-Utility overview".

For the purposes of our leadership discussion we use terms more familiar to leaders. For example:

- We will use "**SELF**" – equates with theory **Self-Utility**
- We will use "**Ask**" – equates with **Directing** or Driving
- We will use "**Act**" – equates with **Action**
- We will use "**Reward**" – equates with **Outcome**

Note that as a theory, Self-Utility is a model and a way of reshaping the way you look at leadership.

Having written the original Theory, an effort was made to make this leadership book more relatable and more readable. In the original <u>Self-Utility: a Theory of Everything</u> terminology of directing, **driving actions to outcomes** was used. In this book and in teaching, **ask act reward** relates more to the basics of leading.

Also, we commonly say "The sun comes up in the morning." Well we all know that the sun doesn't really "come up". In the original theory it would be said that the horizon rotates with the Earth making our sun visible. This book will say "the sun comes up in the morning."

"Discovery consists in seeing what everybody else has seen and thinking what nobody else has thought." – Albert Szent-Gyorgyi (credited with discovering Vitamin C)

3

REMAKING YOURSELF

"Do unto others as you would have others do unto you."
– Bible, Luke 6:31

This "Golden Rule" is not only Christian but a common foundation of many of our world's religions, almost universal. Think about it. The foundation of this teaching is YOU. How would you like others to act toward YOU? Although this might seem self-evident, it is profound in that it forms the foundation of most all our behavior. Yes, we know how we want to be treated, but it still deserves serious reflection and contemplation. That is what this chapter is about.

If you walk into a bookstore you can find a whole section on personal development. This is well and good, but this chapter will only outline a few concepts that have the potential to make really big changes in the quality of who you are.

> *Go to a bookstore and browse the Self-Development section. See if there is something there that fits your needs. Some of my favorites are:*
>
> - *Even Eagles Need a Push by David McNally (good for self assessment)*
> - *The One Minute Manager by Ken Blanchard (good for new leaders or people managing larger number of geographically dispersed)*
> - *The Power of Habit by Charles Duhigg*

You are a product of Nature and Nurture

Certainly Nature endows us with certain physical characteristics that enable and limit our physical abilities as we grow. We are born with certain behavioral patterns that are particularly helpful early in life, but many of these patterns carry over to our later life as well.

Nurture is provided during our upbringing by our parents, our siblings, other relatives, our communities, our institutions and our culture. These nurture attributes come from affiliations which guide our behaviors leading to the core essence of our being.

Both the nature of inheritance and the nurture of all the people and groups that have influenced us have made us into this core essence of being – what we will call our Self-Utility.

*Think about and **list** people that most influenced your life. How did each of these people make you a better person?*

*1.*_____

How?

*2.*_____

How?

*3.*_____

How?

*4.*_____

How?

It takes a community to raise a child – *Hillary Clinton*

At one time, many years ago my Boy Scout Troop helped to raise me. Our troop was getting involved in the discussion of national politics. At the time, Richard Nixon and John F. Kennedy were having debates to help voters determine who our next President of the United States should be.

My two adult troop leaders decided to conduct a mock debate within us scouts. One leaders was a gruff type guy with a raspy voice. He also had a laugh and a smile that made you smile just looking at him. Our other advisor also had a great grin which came most often when he saw one of the scouts do a good deed or do something on their own initiative. After explaining what was going to happen they chose two of us to represent the debaters and the others to assist and give opinions. They chose one of my best friends to speak in the role of Richard Nixon and chose me to speak in the role of John F. Kennedy. We were then each given a week to think and prepare our remarks.

Now consider that this was a Presbyterian sponsored scout troop so it was predictable that they may be biased against a Catholic presidential candidate. I soon approached my two adult leaders to explain how unfair that was. When I approached them they both expressed surprise that I was reluctant to participate as John F. Kennedy. After teasing just a little, they took me aside and explained that this was about learning to take either perspective that life hands you and drawing experience and growth from the experience. Well, I still wasn't satisfied so I went home and complained to my father. He listened but also took their side, in a fatherly way, still insisting that I accept the challenge.

Well, I ended up giving it a shot. The majority, as expected supported my friend as Richard Nixon. It wasn't until a month later, when John F. Kennedy won the election, that I realized that there absolutely was good reason for John F. Kennedy to be the next leader our country. He became one of our best presidents. I realized that my attitude had kept me from making the good arguments and represent the platform that elected our next President. I also got my first strong clue that this was my life, and that I was going to be the product of many people granting me many opportunities. People in my community would also support my positive efforts as I would try new things and I would support the efforts of others as well.

Thank you to my adult troop leaders for helping to raise me. I learned the importance of trying new things assisted by your positive encouragement.

Who have you become as a benefit of others who raised you?

People have helped you along the way to become the person you are today. Now, at this stage in your life it is up to you to do the same for others. But before you do, consider "Who are you?"

Let's continue with a serious introspection of who we are now and who we want to become. This basis will help us to direct our moral imperative (The Golden Rule) toward others. We do so not to force our values upon the rest of the world but rather to reach out to others to share possibilities.

We cannot change the behavior of others unless we have the ability to change our own behavior. This must be the foundation upon which leadership is built. If we do not understand how to change ourselves, how can we possibly change others? If we have not experienced the process of change in our own self, how can we understand the process of change in others? If we do not have a clear vision of who we want to be, how can we understand what others want to be?

Ask yourself and list below your greatest strengths, improvements that you would like to make and opportunities that are open and unique to you (what would you like to change that you can?)

List your greatest strengths:

1._____

2._____

3._____

Other strengths:

Here are a few Leadership Strengths that other authors have considered:

- Committed
- Persistence
- Optimistic
- Enthusiastic
- Good Listener
- Good Motivator
- Tactful
- Appreciative

- Friendly
- Recognize effort
- Organized
- Dependable
- Speaking voice and ability
- Caring and Empathetic
- Focused
- Strategic Thinking/Planning

List things you would like to improve about yourself:

1._____

2._____

Other improvements:

List the opportunities you have to change that you can?

1._____

2._____

3._____

Other opportunities:

Think about what you can change and what you cannot change. Ask other people what they think your strengths are and what they think about your opportunities.

SPEAKING IN PUBLIC GROUPS

Public Speaking is the one strength you will need to develop even if you don't have it now (listening is the other). Speaking to large audiences is something a leader needs to do. It is said that the only fear greater than speaking in public is going to the dentist. How about you?

"I believe that anyone can conquer fear by doing the things he fears to do."
                                                                    - Eleanor Roosevelt

To be a great leader you don't have to be a great speaker, but you will have to give speeches. As Eleanor Roosevelt encourages, if this is a fear of yours, just do it - practice. A great way to practice speaking with positive input is to join a local Toastmasters Club. By speaking under these circumstances you are developing your speaking skill by "asking" yourself to attend, speaking, and then being evaluated and making adjustments accordingly. Repeating these cycles will improve your ability and comfort level.

If you are given a leadership position you can learn to speak on the job. Start with one short speech about the vision you carry for the organization. Tell the story, paint the picture, appeal to the passions your audience has for what they do.

One way to begin speaking if you are really uncomfortable is to write your speech on paper. Practice reading it. Then read it as a speech to the group. This can work in a positive way in that it sends the message that you care so much about them, and your job, that you are willing to give it the extra thought by writing it. After reading a few short speeches you will easily transition to speaking on your own.

ACCEPTING THE CHALLENGE! **Commitment**

"If it is to be, it is up to me."
– William H. Johnson

When you think about the miraculous odds that enabled your very existence, you can't help being in awe of future possibilities that are even yet unseen. Of course, along with these unseen futures lie a myriad of possibilities. Which future will you choose?

WHAT GIVES MEANING TO YOUR LIFE?

If we do not have a noble cause, purpose or direction for our lives, how can we impose cause, purpose and direction on others? If we do not know the meaning of our lives, how can we know the meaning of other's lives? How can we know what behaviors can produce the outcomes we so deeply desire?

These questions are not just philosophical - they are real and relevant. A leader is constantly seeking these answers. However, total understanding of individual's human nature should not keep us from beginning our leadership quest. Be attentive. These things are learned as you move forward, relating to each other. Meeting other's needs, wants and fears can empower you and them to fulfillment of dreams. Get started now; learn as you go.

A few pages ago we reflected on "the people that influenced your life and who you became as a result". Now let's look ahead at your future.

What are the main thing(s) you would like to ask yourself to change?

1._____

Other changes:

Now try to do one of these. Ask your family and friends for positive support to help you.

MYERS-BRIGGS PERSONALITY PROFILE - stepping outside your comfort zone

Sitting in a Creative Management class at the University of Notre Dame twenty years ago, we were studying the Myers Briggs Personality Profile assessment. Before we got into the explanations of how it worked, we all took the multiple-choice fill-in-the-dot test ourselves.

At the next session, I had an epiphany of understanding. Among a lot of other explanations with charts, graphs, evidence and support, the lecturer hit on something that changed my life. The presenter explained that our personalities as an outcome from this test reflected our "comfort zone" personality. We were likely to be not only better in these modes but they also indicated our personality. An important point was that even though we did need to spend **most** of our time in these "comfort zones", we should **not** be spending **all** of our time there!

He followed with a strong suggestion that we are to step outside of these zones from time to time in order to try on new personality types, to grow and to add these behavior patterns to our skill sets. It was so simple, but yet so profound. Yes, regardless of our given personalities we could try on new personalities for a short time. By repeating this "stepping out" on occasion, we would vastly expand our potential for living our dream, for exacting a cause, or for becoming a leader!

Being an analytical introvert, I spent most of my life observing and learning about people and how they think. After this new revelation I started stepping outside my comfort zone from time to time by being more outgoing, and shaking hands and taking initiative to talk with people. In addition, "stepping out" seemed to make me less judgmental about people and more empathetic to their perspective and emotion in the decision-making process. My introverted personality, which I retained, became redirected at will, and molded me into being a very good listener.

Consider taking a personality profile on your own. There are a number of different types both by professionals and outlined in books

- *Myers-Briggs Personality Profile*
- *True Colors Personality Test by Lowry*
- *Newcastle Personality Assessor by Nettle*

MENTORSHIP Colleagues, Friends, partners, spouses

"Our greatest need in life is to have someone
who will make us do what we can."
– Unknown

My mentor in leadership was Dr. Phil VanDenBerg. When I was first elected President of our local Optimist Club, I heard that he had been on the nomination committee and recommended me. As it happened, he was to be our next State Governor for the Optimists at the same time I was the local president. We both recognized the opportunity. He could help me by teaching me about leadership and I could help him with the success of the state organization. We both worked hard for eighteen months and got to know each other very well. We became best friends and mentored each other through upper level jobs with Optimist International. Tragically, he died unexpectedly about fifteen years later at the age of fifty-one.

The knowledge and skills I acquired during our relationship gave me the ability to later become both the President of Optimist International as well as the President of Voluntary Optometric Services to Humanity – International.

Being mentored (and mentoring others) is one of the most effective ways of changing your behavior, your habits, and can potentially even evolve your values and personality.

If you anticipate taking a leadership position, seek out someone who has been successful at the job, office or position you anticipate. It is best if you really like the person who could become your mentor. Begin by inviting them to lunch or dinner and talk about your common interests. Mentorships can be more productive if you spend significant time with the mentor such as conferences or retreats. Conversation can then extend to almost any topic, giving surprising insights and understanding.

Mentorship from within the organization is excellent. If you have a superior or officer above you, consider the option of using them as a mentor. Many organizations are designed to do this anyway.

Mentorship can be a more generic relationship toward general life skills or it can be very specific toward organizations, family life, career, self-development, leadership, spiritual growth or any other areas of interest. Mentorship often involves various levels of expertise, or may involve two people of similar levels of experience. A primary outcome is reciprocal relationship building.

Guidelines for your mentor:

- Have knowledge or skill sets you admire
- Be someone you would enjoy being around
- Be nearby or accessible

Write down your current or most recent mentor(s). How did you benefit from the relationship?

> *Write down three people that you would like to ask for a future mentoring relationship. Why?*
>
> 1._____
>
> 2._____
>
> 3._____

Although you may not list them in this exercise, always value your spouse or partner in life as being a great mentor.

CHANGING AN ACTION INTO A HABIT – toward who you become

> *Keep your thoughts positive – thoughts become your words.*
> *Keep your words positive – words become your behaviors.*
> *Keep your behavior positive – behavior become your habits.*
> *Keep your habits positive – habits become your values.*
> *Keep your values Positive – values become your destiny.*

> ■ *Mahatma Gandhi, Open Your Mind, Open Your Life*

How do you change "who" you are?

The answer is "It's the same way that you eat an Elephant – one bite at a time."

1. Decide what you will do and how you will reward yourself.
2. Reach deep inside yourself to make the commitment – own it.

3. "Just do it". Do the action and give yourself a reward each time.

Do this action a hundred times and it becomes a Behavior.

Do this action five hundred times and it becomes a Habit.

Do this action a thousand times and it becomes part of your Personality.

Do this action thousands of times and it becomes "Who" you are!

Psychologists and Leaders have shown how behaviors that are repeated can evolve into new identities. Eventually your behaviors become automatic – you no longer have to consciously decide to act. This means that you are on your way to a better you.

Pick another action/behavior that you would like to change and "go for it"!

This is the basis of how you use the "Cycle of Influence" as a feedback loop on yourself. Change occurs by your "directives" driving your "actions/behaviors" toward a positive "outcome". **Ask act reward** with determination (repetition) gets the job done!

A Couple of Notes on Changing Habits:

- "Triggers" can elicit a responsive action. It is helpful to find something that reminds you of your intended behavior – something that elicits the behavior.
- Give yourself a small reward after a positive action. This can elicit a positive feeling. Think small rewards for small actions, large rewards for major behaviors.
- Work toward the point where the cycle is automatic; you don't have to think about actions, they just happen.

Apply the four-part cyclical feed-back loop that leads to change.

Fig 1 Cycle of Influence

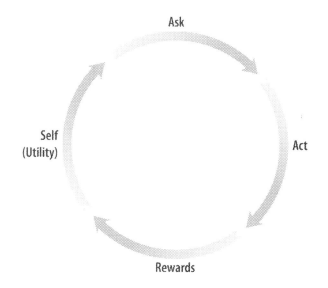

Cycle of Influence

SUMMARY OF THIS CHAPTER:

- *Change is a given. You are the product of everything and everyone who changed you into who you are today. Your change today will determine who you will be tomorrow.*

- *Take an inventory of who you are. Write down who you want to become.*

- *Spend time with a mentor or two. This is the easiest way to repeat a lot of feed-back loops of "Cycles of Influence" to change behavior into habit.*

- *Write down and carry a description of the person you would like to be.*

Accept the Challenge! Take control and "own" your future. It may not be easy but it can remake you into the person you deserve to be.

4

CYCLES OF INFLUENCE

Understanding and using these feed-back loops or cycles can give you control of change, not only in your own life, but also in others. These three diagrams represent a single entity individual, group or idea/cause.

STEP by STEP THROUGH the FOUR STAGES of the CYCLE

A) How an <u>INDIVIDUAL</u> "cycle of influence" works

"<u>CYCLE OF INFLUENCE</u>" is a feed-back loop of the process by which a Self (Utility), or Group/Organization (Utility) effects change. This cycle represents the self or group driving/Ask which in turn drives action/behavior which results in outcomes/reward which feeds back modification to its self or group.

SELF-UTILITY

Fig 2 Self-Utility

Cycle of Influence

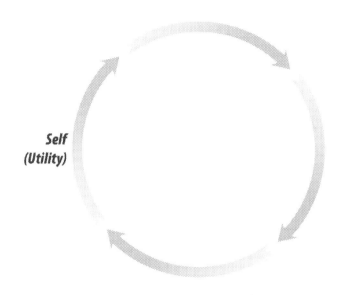

Self
(Utility)

We begin with <u>SELF</u> (Utility). In human terms it is the core of your being, "who you are". This broad definition also includes survival instinct, character, personality, self-image, self-interest, selfishness, drive, Ego and will power – it is generally subconscious.

Note that each of these four labels represents a "general" or "global" definition. Therefore to be more specific, terminology may change with each situation being discussed.

DIRECTIVE

Fig 3 Directive (Ask)

Cycle of Influence

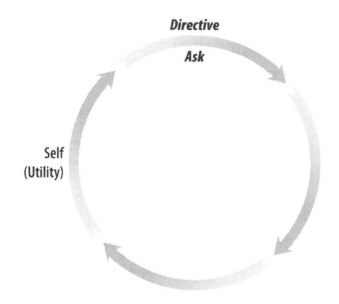

Next in the outward expression of Self (Utility) is the DIRECTIVE (Ask). This is the intention, mission, vision, purpose, plan, objective, moral imperatives (ethics, morals, loyalty, allegiance and respect), dreams, desires, and aims. Note that these "directives/ drives" are expressed a little differently for groups.

Keep in mind a subtle difference, moral imperatives (ethics, morals, loyalty, allegiance and respect) are those qualities revealed by observed actions or behaviors, not necessary by what is spoken. "Judge a tree by the fruit it bears, not by the fruit it talks about".

ACTIONS (Act)

Fig 4 Actions

Cycle of Influence

Directives (Ask) lead to ACTIONS which are the flashpoint of where change occurs. ACTIONS are generally observable and measurable. ACTIONS can also be called behavior, accomplishment, achievement, deed, incident, clash, incident, event and encounter.

Note that technically a thought is an ACTION which can have an outcome cycling into another thought. For example consider shooting a basketball through a hoop. Sometimes mental imaging can make a positive impact on our performance.

<u>OUTCOMES</u> (rewards)

Fig 5 Outcomes

Cycle of Influence

Following any action are <u>OUTCOMES</u> or rewards from the action. This is commonly thought of in psychology as you feeling pleasure or pain. A sub-set of OUTCOMES include Impact, evaluation, the effect on emotion, mood or feeling.

FEED-BACK TO SELF-UTILITY

The important part of this CYCLE is that the OUTCOMEs feed back into the original SELF which on each cycle makes a change – sometimes imperceptible but with multiple repetitions may be significant!

This then represents an Individual's CYCLE OF INFLUENCE (feed-back loop). It shows how your SELF can

cause change. **And as to our definition of LEADERSHIP, the greater the change and the greater the number of people, the greater the leader!**

B) How a <u>GROUP</u> "cycle of influence" works

Groups can be formal or informal. They can be social or institutional. They can be:

- Family – Households, Extended Families
- Educational - Schools, Class Mates
- Social – Neighborhoods, Communities, Peers, Fraternal Societies
- Business – Co-workers, Management, Boards of Directors
- Professional Organizations
- Service Organizations – Clubs, Leagues
- Governmental - Township, City, County, State, Country, United Nations

Fig 6 Group

Cycle of Influence

A <u>GROUP-UTILITY</u> is the same. But in group terms it takes on a social-political character. The broad definition would more likely include terms such as constitution, purpose, network, sustainability, group-image and presence and a common bond.

Note that the group (group-utility) unit is made of components parts, that is, a number of individual selves. This, of course, is not unique, in that everything in the universe is made up of component parts, even the self.

DIRECTIVES: Drive, Institutions, Loyalty, Respect, Affiliation, Accountability, Traditions, Charters, Rituals, ideology - **ask** is a verbal specific expression of one of these

ACTIONS: Conventions, Conferences, Telecommunication, Speeches, Working, Selling, Manufacturing – **act** is a specific action

OUTCOMES: Recognition, Evaluation, Product appreciation, Sales increase, Morale Climbs – **reward** is a specific outcome. These feed back to SELF-UTILITY as a better self-image.

C) How an <u>IDEA or CAUSE</u> "cycle of influence" works

Fig 7 Cause

An <u>idea-utility</u> or cause-utility has the same dynamics. By being an idea, the cycle exists as a thought carried by a number of people or perhaps even a process held in the minds of people or in cyber space. These Self-Utilities might include causes, ideas, movements or theories.

SUMMARY: This describes a **SINGLE** "CYCLE OF INFLUENCE" is – this feed-back loop represents change within itself. In reality, of course, it is simulated and evolves through contact with other people and things.

Next we will explore how these single "CYCLES OF INFLUENCE" are connected to and react with other people and things.

5

CHANGING OTHERS

CHANGING BEHAVIOR OF KILLER WHALES

Have you ever watched the killer whales" at Sea World perform? It is incredible what these powerful creatures can do as they jump out of the water through a hoop to the amazement of hundreds. Well, how does one get the whale to do that?

To make this change in the whale the trainer begins by placing a rope at the bottom of their pool. If the whale accidentally swims over it the trainer gives the whale food - a fish as a reward. The rope is them moved a few inches off the bottom and if the whale swims over it, the trainer gives them another fish as a reward. The rope is again raised, and continually raised to the surface while all the time the trainer rewards them with a fish. Of course at this point the whale is actually jumping out of the water to obtain the food reward. Soon the rope becomes a ring and the whale jumps out of the water and through the ring to the wonder and amazement of audiences. And the trainers still give them the reward.

Fig 8 Trainer interacting with Whale

Cycles of Influence

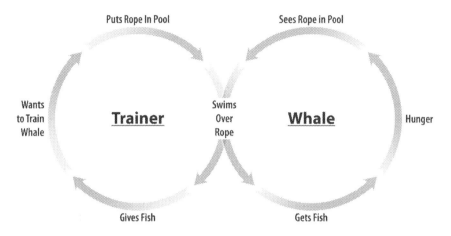

Of course people are not whales and you would not give them a fish as a reward. We know that our followers are not this simple, nor are they as easy to mold behavior. This illustration may seem trite, but it serves as one of the simplest demonstrations of how great change occurs by repeating this simple cycle of influence – trainer wants whale to jump through hoops (since the "ask" cannot be made opportunity is) > trainer lays rope on bottom of pool > whale swims over rope (act) > whale fed fish (reward)> whale motivated to swim over rope again.

A) __TWO PEOPLE__ interacting with "cycles of influence"

Now we will take a look at how two "Cycles of Influence" interact, causing change. Remember that the "flashpoint" of change occurs at the point of contact between the two – behavior.

Let's start with seeing how

ONE SALES PERSON INTERACTS WITH A PROSPECTIVE CUSTOMER

Fig 9 Person with Customer

SALES PERSON WITH A PROSPECTIVE CUSTOMER:

Sitting and enjoying a great cup of coffee in a mall, I am distracted by a young man across the hall in his twenties changing the behavior of dozens of people as they walk through the hotel corridor. He is good-looking, dressed in a youthful but stylish black suit with a silver belt buckle. He is wearing an open collar purple shirt. His hair is stylish with a well coiffed beard. He also has a great smile adaptable to the potential of the passerby.

He represents a cosmetic store and his goal is to make cosmetic sales by enticing walkers into the store - somewhat like a circus barker enticing people into a circus tent.

So, his presumed intent is to get people to come into the store to purchase products. He does this by setting up a series of "cycles of influence" targeted on behavior - the flash-point of change is interaction.

He does this by first initiating a relationship by establishing early eye contact and an alluring smile with women as they approach from down the hall. About half the time their behavior is altered as they stop or pause when he reaches out to offer them a small but tasteful black bag with silver engraving (reward). *Cycle of influence one is complete as his smile and offer results in a change of behavior in the walker as they slow and stop.*

He next gives them attention by talking with them. If they start to leave he gives them another free sample from a basket nearby and they pause. *Cycle two is complete with this step.*

Then the next behavior is to get them to walk into the store where a cosmetic person tailors the customer's interests and needs to specific cosmetic products. *Cycle three of behavior modification is complete.*

Finally the customer finds something she wants. The sale is made. She walks away with a faint smile and the store makes a sale. Both are happy. *Thus cycle four achieves the overall objective to the encounter.*

Persistence paid off. It is also interesting to notice that in reality only some are even targeted. As people walk toward the salesperson he obviously makes a prediction of his success by the way they look and walk. He only appeals to about half of the people with his smile and invitation. Of those approached, less than half respond. Even a smaller number make a purchase.

So even if this works on only five percent of the passers-by, the store succeeds. Of course the expertise and outcomes of the sales staff can greatly influence the outcomes of moving through these interactive "cycles of influence" effectively.

B. An Individual (Board Member) working within a GROUP (Foundation)

Fig 10 Member in Organization

Cycles of Influence

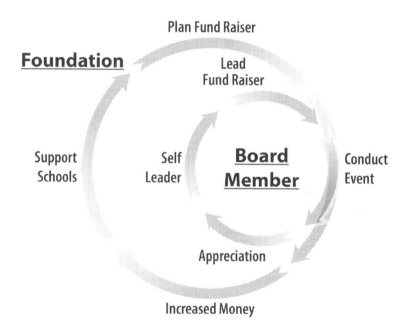

These cycles of influence illustrate a board member working within the greater group of the foundation to change the foundation and themselves by raising money. Working within the context of a group is a basic way for leadership to be expressed. The cycles share so much in common (purpose, participation and outcomes – Ask, Act, Reward) that the work of all is leveraged positively to success.

This foundation has a purpose to help local students within the local school system have a quality education experience. The foundation has used most of its funds to add a cyber café in the local high school which was very well received by the students.

The foundation now needs a fundraising project to raise more money for a teacher assistance program. The foundation board decides to conduct a "silent auction." The president then asks an individual board member to be the chairperson to plan and conduct the project. She accepts and has the "silent auction" with assistance from the board members resulting in raising $7,000 in funds for the teacher project. The teacher assistance program is implemented.

Consider how a pebble falling in water spreads throughout the pond. This ripple effect is how our actions ripple through our spheres of influence as they impact others. A leader is one who can harness this rippling change by directing collective behaviors toward organizational, social and cultural change. The potential is almost limitless.

CHANGING MANY PEOPLE – LEADERSHIP

Are you ready to lead? Consider your innermost being - what you want, what you need, what is your passion, "How could you make your community a better place?" Consider change in the context of your relationship with cycles that drive actions, behaviors and outcomes.

Are you ready to lead?

What is your calling? What is your Passion?

How could you make your Community a better place? Why?

Make a list of things you could do to influence this change:

This exercise is a way to brainstorm some possible options that your leadership could impact. Once you have some ideas down look around to see what groups or causes you might join to realize your purpose.

SPHERES OF INFLUENCE – Bringing People Together

"SPHERE OF INFLUENCE" is a generic term to represent the many Cycles of Influence around itself, creating a sphere (like atoms with electrons around its nucleus). These cycles and spheres can expand to make connections to other groups and other selves. That would represent the extent to which our influence will reach.

This "Sphere of Influence" is where we transition to "APPLIED LEADERSHIP". By applying a "functional" approach to leadership we expand our own "Sphere of Influence". As we begin to understand outcomes, we will learn how to change outcomes – first in small ways, and with experience, greater and greater control will be within our reach.

As we come to the end of Part One, we have considered a different approach to Leadership – one that is directed toward outcomes (rewards). People and results change at the flashpoint of interacting, where our Spheres of Influence touch and connect with each another. A well directed focus can impact results, cumulatively in a big way.

Along the leadership path, a leader has many interactions. Most will go well - many won't. Our attitude is what can get us through. Our attitude can find something positive in failure. Our attitude can be an inspiration to others. Our attitude will make our work enjoyable.

> *Every test in our life makes us bitter or better,*
> *Every problem comes to break us or make us.*
> *The choice is ours whether to become victim or victor.*

> *– Unknown*

LEAD by Driving Actions to Outcomes
Ask, Act, Reward

Based on THEORY OF SELF-UTILITY with an
Emphasis on Non-Profits from Local to International

PART TWO

APPLIED LEADERSHIP

6

INTRODUCTION TO
APPLIED LEADERSHIP

So you have the background and you probably have some experiences being a leader – some of you more than others. Do not discount all that you have already learned from those experiences and people you've known in your life. No book can ever teach you those lessons with the intensity of living them - lessons you've learned both from your successes and from your failures. You have a certain potential for being a leader because of them.

But you have not reached a destination. You are only at a point in your "journey of life". Where do you want to go next?

In the first part of this book we have explored the basics of a new, but really effective leadership theory. In the first part you have reviewed some basics about yourself – "who you are" and "what you want to do, or change".

In this second part we are going to show some ways you can be effective in all stages of leadership. You will learn the step-by-step methods of changing the actions of many people toward a greater outcome, an outcome greater than yourself and them.

Part two explains techniques of leading within the group context. Chapters are loosely organized by the four stages of the "Cycle of

Influence." The terminology will change accordingly to approximate the Group dynamics:

- Self-Utility: Constitution, Bylaws, Purpose and Culture
- Directives: Ask, Mission, Policies, Objectives and Goals
- Actions: Meetings, Service outreach, Growth and Communication
- Outcomes: Rewards, Recognition, Impact, Evaluation, Result

Joining a group offers a leader a great opportunity to leverage their influence and offers power to make change. A group has a common cycle of influence since members within the group share many of the same values and causes. Joining together not only creates strong bond among people but adds strength to their ability to make change. That inter-connection also allows them to leverage their influence to a result greater than its parts.

Note: These discussions have attempted to make your approach simple. It is geared more toward "volunteer" or "non-profit" organizations. Terms used, suggestions made and "to-do" lists are guidelines to be used more as a checklist of possibilities rather than a mandate. As it remains simple, realize that there are always exceptions that may fit your circumstances better.

Also Note: Changes in others are gradual and small, not usually sudden and profound. The objective in leadership is to mold people to meet their aspirations while achieving your vision – shared goals.

7

ACT LIKE A LEADER
TO BE A LEADER

A Group Cheer: **"To <u>Be</u> enthusiastic we must <u>Act</u> enthusiastic!"**

Repeat this over and over, louder and louder

This is a simple exercise to use in a large group to get "fired up"! The point is that enthusiasm is a great motivator. It is infectious, it spreads. It is what others want. And, as a leader, it begins with YOU!

But an equally important observation is that this simple "cheer" is our theory applied. You can <u>be</u> what you <u>do</u>. This is profound. As a leader you must **act** like a leader and by **acting** like a leader you **become** a leader – simple, right? Okay then, let's begin.

Michael Angelo Caruso is a much-in-demand motivational speaker and author. What drew me to him was his ability to change people's actions in such simple ways that they could walk out of his seminars with positively changed behaviors. For example, he would teach "how to shake hands."

How to shake a person's hand:

Place the web of your hand (between your thumb and index finger) firmly into the web of the other hand. Shake firmly.

Follow by looking into their eyes and smiling.

A handshake, what a way to make a great impression? What a simple action that is to build a relationship! I would always marvel at the people coming out of his seminars enthusiastically practicing this newly learned "hand shake" technique.

Other short behaviors to build relationships:

- *Greeting people by Name*
- *Asking people their opinion*
- *Listening intently*
- *Asking them questions*
- *Giving people an honest compliment*
- *Looking people in the eye*
- *Smiling*

Other easily learned behaviors to "walk-the-walk" and "talk-the-talk" of a leader:

- *Walk into a room with your head held high and your shoulders back*
- *Take the initiative of saying "hello" to people (handshake above)*
- *Sit on the center isle or at the front of the room*
- *Learn to tell a story and a non-offensive joke*
- *Put your arm over the chair next to you (if vacant)*
- *Give nods of approval during a speech*
- *At a reception, look for someone not engaged and talk with them*
- *Smile*
- *See Books on other "Body Language" techniques*

"To <u>Be</u> a Leader, you must <u>Act</u> like a Leader!"

The best testimonial for "act like a leader" is toward the end of a "Ted Talk" called "Your Body Language" by Amy Cuddy. She recalls her and a colleague's experience with "Fake it 'till you make it."

8

ACCEPTING THE CHALLENGE

Previously we have considered techniques to change ourselves and how to build relationships. We've also learned the basics of ask act reward. Now we are ready to apply our self-inventory toward serving within a group or organization. We are ready to accept a challenge.

How could you make the world a better place? Consider that a greater purpose may exist for you. And that it may have something to do with the meaning of life. You may not know what that is yet. As you change and grow re-visit this concept of a greater purpose from time to time. As the influence of your leadership grows, think about the impact you are making with others – and to what purpose.

WHY DO WE DO WHAT WE DO? (Maslow's Hierarchy of Needs) Higher to Lower

- Physiological needs – food, clothing, shelter
- Safety needs – security, lack of fear
- Social needs – friends, fitting in with others
- Esteem needs, respect, appreciation
- Self-Actualization – realizing individual potential

Do you know yourself well enough to know why you do what you do?

Remember our earlier discussion of actions and behaviors? This not only was the flashpoint of change but it was also observable and measurable. Try making a log of your activities over the next few days and see where you spend your time. Does this match up with your hierarchy of needs? Does this fit with your internal motivation?

As a leader, try this exercise by observing others. Observing how they spend their time can be a great way to tell what their hierarchy is and what motivates them. In other words, it is more insightful to assess values by what people do than by what people say.

As you consider accepting your challenge ahead think about what really motivates you and how you can activate yourself. Improving yourself doesn't mean jumping to the top of the hierarchy, but perhaps nudging yourself up to the next level.

Your success as a leader will also be enhanced by understanding others and what their needs are. You may be able to give others a great gift by working together to a greater purpose.

"You make a living by what you get; you make a life by what you give."
– Winston Churchill (unconfirmed)

As you accept the challenge you make a commitment to yourself that you have the attitude, dedication and persistence to improve the world for others in some way.

"Administer" is from Latin meaning "to help others".
It's more about them than it is about you.

9

BUILDING RELATIONSHIPS

– BRINGING "SPHERES OF INFLUENCE" TOGETHER

As we transition into expanding the reach of leadership we consider "spheres of influence" as to how far our sphere of influence reaches.

As we discuss a wide variety of cycles of influence, we can assume that many other cycles are revolving around the same Self-Utility at the same time. Imagine these many cycles forming a spheres – like electrons revolving around their nucleus.

Spheres (Individuals) close together – stronger connection means a potential relationship

These represent two people who know each other but don't have much in common. They may meet in a restaurant and exchange a social greeting. That could be the beginning of forming a relationship if pursued.

Fig 11 Two spheres apart

Spheres of Influence

If one says to the other, "hey let's have lunch next Tuesday" and the other accepts, their lunch together would bring them together to interact by actually touching each other's sphere of influence.

Fig 12 Two Spheres Together

Spheres of Influence

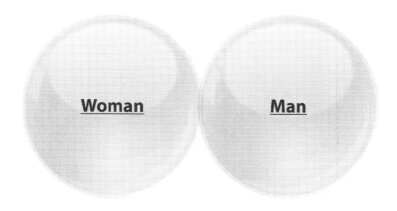

Some Individuals have more influential spheres than others. A powerful leader has a larger sphere as her influence is expansive.

Ways to bring a Relationship together:

- *Ask someone to lunch*
- *Call them on the phone*
- *Shake their hand*
- *Smile at them, say hello*
- *Give them your business card*
- *Add them as a "friend" on social media site (FaceBook)*
- *Introduce them to a friend (bringing three cycles together)*
- *Write them a "thank-you" note*

Later – ways to nurture a relationship

Larger (Group) Sphere of Influence interacting with smaller (individual) sphere

A group's sphere of influence then is larger and more influential than an individual's sphere. It reaches more people and has more influence.

Consider the large sphere below representing a group and the smaller sphere representing an individual. If separated they have no connection and therefore little influence on each other.

Fig 13 Group sphere and individual sphere apart

Spheres of Influence

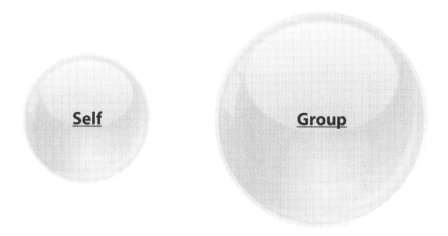

Now consider that the two spheres of influence come close together and connect. That connection creates an interaction between the two, changing each in some way – sometimes imperceptible and sometime profound.

The real power of groups is that your affiliation or membership in them is the quickest and most efficient way to boost your sphere of influence. Together, people can do more!

Fig 14 Group Sphere and Individual Sphere together

Spheres of Influence

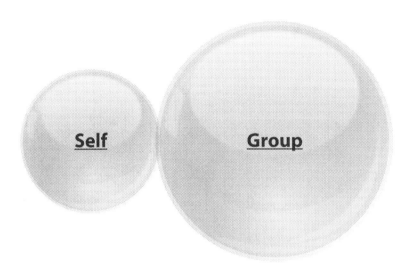

Bringing our spheres of influence together is a life-long step. As you build relationships through networking, you are building your Influence as a leader. As you work with an organization, you are leveraging your Leadership impact.

Maintaining Relationships

Your ongoing relationship will naturally grow. As you lead, inspire, and manage outcomes, remember that it must always be done with respect and courtesy. People have other priorities that may keep them from contributing. If they can't do the job they signed up for, make it easy for them to step back. Appreciate and empathize with their perspective.

Sending personal hand-written cards is a good way to build and maintain relationships. So many things are electronically generated that the personal touch can show that you care.

If you have a large number of relationships, consider the following effective, time-saving way to send birthday cards:

Sending Personal Birthday Cards:

1. *Purchase Cards/Envelopes (with your Logo/Theme?) and appropriate stamps.*
2. *Address all the envelopes and put their birth (Month/day) where the stamp goes. Put them in shoeboxes or a file with the envelope showing the date (upper right) in order.*
3. *Every week remove the cards/envelops, stamp them, write nice, short notes, seal and mail them.*

You may want to do two years (two sets) worth of Cards if applicable.

Relationship Building with your new Officers or Committee Appointees

The basics are early contact for "congratulations" soon after the election or appointment. And a welcome might begin with talking about them and their families or special interests. It's also good to talk about anything you might already have in common. The first visit or phone call might also be about sharing contact information, calendar dates and such.

This is followed by basic information of job description and expectations.

Relationship building is not only important for working relationships, but it often becomes the beginning of deep, lasting friendships.

Relationship building is very personal and quite diverse in the way that it is expressed. As a frame of reference, consider that relationship building is ongoing and interwoven into the fabric of leadership and service. Therefore we are going to continue relationship building as an ongoing integral part of leadership.

The ultimate benefit of relationship building is to understand what that new officer/appointee wants or needs from the job ahead. The process of leadership is to make both of your dreams come true while making the organization grow.

10

ASSETS AND RESOURCES

Any good leader learns to understand the people as well as the infrastructure of the organization.

People are most any organization's greatest asset. They are what drive your organization. They are the vital force that moves your organization toward success. People also hold the culture of the organization – the unwritten rules for behavior and belonging.

Organization leaders include but are not limited to Chief Executive Officers, other officers, staff, members, owners, stakeholders, and board members. People are the "brick and mortar" of an organization.

If people are the "brick and mortar", Incorporation Papers, Constitution, Bylaws and Policies are the "infra structure". They define the group, "Who the group is" and "What they do". The group is also defined by the laws of governments within their jurisdiction.

Most of this Book is about people because people make change. But just as it is important to know the people, it is essential that you know the organization's structure and rules.

Corporate Papers, Bylaws and Policies

Corporate papers are generally pretty basic and have to do with the type of corporation you are in. They do include the names of officers and directors. It is a matter of course to change officers and directors as per bylaws. Knowing who is "in charge" can help you understand the organization.

Bylaws generally hold the core purposes, objectives, governance and protocol of the organization. They often have to do with meetings, elections, finance, membership and programs – all big, basic stuff.

Policies are rules determined by the board of directors. Ideally they would include policies of "means" (what we want done) and "limits" (what resources we can allocate).

Knowing the structure is helpful to every member as a base of operations. It is essential for a leader to know them in that they define the playing field on which they operate. Knowledge is power. And knowledge of the corporate papers, bylaws and policies is power when leading. It's not good to tout your knowledge, but it gives you great credibility when you cite a passage to get the board through a difficult situation. It has been amazing how boards get trapped into going around and around on issues when guidelines for dealing with the issue are already built into the structure.

Changing Bylaws and Policy

Changing policy is usually a simple majority vote of the board of directors. If you are a voting board member, do your research and vote analytically. If you are not a voting member, let one know of your input and opinion. Changing bylaws is usually a bit more restrictive, institutional and constant.

Before you set out to change bylaws it is good to have some experience and deep understanding of the purposes and culture of the organization. Understand the rationale of the bylaws and policies and how they work.

Change can be very helpful to an organization. What better impact can leader have if not to change the core structure if needed? But remember, bylaws and policies are there for a reason, so if you think a benefit exists by changing them, consider some guidelines first.

Guidelines for changing Bylaws or Policies:

- *Do you understand the organizational outcome of the change?*
- *List the costs and benefits of implementation.*
- *Are you a good analytical, strategic thinker?*
- *Where will you get your support for voting?*

If everything is truly in alignment, changing bylaws is one of the best, lasting ways to change an organization – and an incredibly powerful way to influence the future.

Note: Sometimes changing a large section of bylaw design can be easier than passing an individual item. Keep this approach in mind considering that groups often spend large amounts of time on small issues (or even individual words), leaving large changes sometimes easier to make.

Note: Bylaws have dynamics that interconnect as if it were an art form. Consider the "Constitution of the United States". This enduring document has been revised many times but retains its relevancy in its entirety – it works as a whole, not just as independent articles.

Information Access – Information is power

Many local organizations are connected to a "parent" organization and if not may identify with others in their area of interest. Either way, there is probably a lot of information available to help your organization be more successful.

- Web-sites: Much of our information today is online. Parent organizations particularly have a huge amount of information to help local affiliates succeed.

    – Contact names, emails for questions and advise
    – Planning guides and materials for new projects
    – Financial information and budget planning
    – Government regulations affecting your organization
    – Online payments and ordering systems
    – Social Media access and sites of interest

- Publications

    – International Bylaws and Policies as well a local model Bylaws/Policies
    – Magazines for general membership
    – Leadership Publications about the Organization
    – Recognition Materials

- Conferences

    – Local or Area Conferences and Seminars for learning
    – Annual Conventions for fun and motivation

Finances and Budget

Dealing with finances is probably not your organizations ultimate goal, unless you are a Foundation. Groups are however, an important tool for getting things done – a means to an end.

Financial management takes disciplined control. If you can't control your finances you become seriously handicapped.

Budgets are a way for the group to plan. They anticipate their income and plan their expenses. Income can be generated internally from dues or contributions; this is usually used for administration. Income can be raised from the community at-large; this is usually returned to the community with programs.

Budgets are interesting in that they are an objective measure of priorities. Look at an organizations balance sheet and see their priorities. As such, this is an analytical exercise in planning.

Budgets are usually created annually, in advance, by the organization's finance chair along with the president (CEO) and treasurer. The treasurer receives income (revenue) and pays out expenses. The finance chairperson checks receipts and statements to make sure all transactions agree with the treasurer's Report – monthly or quarterly.

<u>Both</u> report their findings to the board. The treasurer and finance chair work in tandem as a "check-and-balance" system to make sure each other are protected as well as the general membership. Fraud and embezzlement, unfortunately happens more often than you might think. Keep it positive; keep it checked.

Foundations

Foundations are usually organized in the United States as a 501c3. This allows donors to make tax deductible gifts. Foundations raise money toward a stated cause or other non-profit organization.

Fund Raising

There is a wide variety of promotions and events organized to raise money. Generally the board of directors approves the proposal and the President appoints a chairperson to organize and conduct the promotion or event.

Best Fund Raisers are:

- *High Income*
- *Low Investment*
- *Minimal Risk*
- *Build Member Morale*
- *Maximize Non-profit's Name Recognition*
- *Short term high profile event*

11

LEADING YOUR TEAM

So you have just been selected as your organization's next Chief Executive Officer (CEO). Ready or not, here you go. You have just been honored. Your organization chose you to lead – be gracious. Charge!

The first step is to write down what you see happening during your tenure. Brainstorm some ideas, events, feelings, prestige, community impact, recognition and outcomes. How will your community be better as a result of your leadership? Later you will convert these into goals.

Lead by Example

Lead by example. This is the purest form of leadership, you act; they do what you do. Setting a positive example by contributing to the group's success gives you credibility for leadership. It is easier to ask someone to do something that you have already done.

Can you motivate someone else?

That is a tough question often proposed by speakers. The answer is often, "No, people can only motivate themselves." I'll agree that is technically correct. But a leader can certainly set the stage, give an incentive, empower with resources and show the way toward action. So yes, if any or all of those things lead to action, I call it "motivation."

Pragmatically, however, motivation isn't the objective of leading – Action is! Action and behavior are observable, empirical and measurable – motivation is not.

This brings us back to our Theory. "Leadership is the ability to change the behaviors (actions) of a large numbers of people toward a predetermined outcome." Always keep this in clear focus.

Charisma and enthusiastic speeches are only a small part of motivation. The power of a leader to change outcomes lies below the surface. Remember the iceberg. The power of an iceberg is in the eighty percent you cannot see – the same with leadership.

"Surround yourself with Leaders that are better than you"

By now you should have a pretty good idea of what your strengths are. Think about what strengths other people have that will complement yours. For example, if you are a serious kind of person, find someone who is funny and can entertain a crowd. Put them in a position to use their strength while benefiting the organization.

Now it's time to direct your attention to recruiting those who will serve with you. Although you probably know them, it would be good to investigate a little deeper into their strengths and interests.

Positions you might be looking for often are secretary, treasurer, officers, board members, committee chairpersons and committee members. Note that some of these are elected, in which case you should be very careful to intercede unless the position goes unfilled.

Consider the following techniques for fitting people with opportunities:

Ways to look for key people:

- *Distribute and invite everyone to fill out an "Interest Finder"**
    - *Include Name and contact information*
    - *Ask for their birthday (not year)*
    - *List Committees or Positions available*
    - *Leave space for "other input"*

- *Interview each person casually to learn about their interests and abilities, and to build a stronger relationship with them.*
- *Past observations may give you some performance indication as well*

A committee is group that will organize and implement an activity, event or serve a generalized ongoing function. A committee is responsible to the board, supervised by the President (CEO).

With this information put together a list of current and new positions (list committees) you will need to achieve the outcome you expect.

Make a Committee Appointment Chart to facilitate your search for chair or committee.

1) Make a chart or spreadsheet of each position that you are looking for.
    a. First Column: list the "job" (such as fund raising chairperson)

    b. Second Column: write #, or number of members needed. Leave more lines under each job than the # you need.

    c. Third Column: list strengths needed for that job (such as outgoing or analytical or dependable or funny)

    d. Fourth Column: enter prospective names (put * next to choice for chair)

    e. Fifth Column: Notes

Make the Appointment

You have just assessed the strengths and interests of everyone on your team. Using the "Cycles of Influence" for each person you will next:

    a. ASK (directive) them to serve a specific job description and expectation

    b. MANAGE (actions/behaviors) their progress with counsel, support, enthusiasm and accountability (they report their progress at every Board Meeting)

    c. REWARD (outcome) their progress and completion

ASK each to serve as a **Committee Chairperson** individually without distractions

"Ask in person, recognize in public"

For each Committee Chair ASK, use this guide:

- *Tell Committee Name and why you are asking them to be chairperson*
  - *Mention special qualities that make them a good choice*

- *Give them the "Job Description" (actions)*
- *Give them your "Expectations" (outcomes)*
- *Tell them of their Resources: (online, planning guides, budget)*
- *Important: Give them "ownership" of this job by coaxing them to tell you:*
  - *What steps need to be done?*
  - *Who will do each step?*
  - *When will each step be done?*

While **asking**, fill out this appointment form. (chair gets copy, President gets copy)

COMMITTEE APPOINTMENT FORM

*Committee*_____*Chair's*

*Name*_____

Job Description:

Expectation (outcome):

Resources:

List steps to completion:

What needs to be done?   Who will do it?   When?

SAMPLE FORM FILLED OUT

COMMITTEE <u>Youth and Community Service</u> **CHAIR**
NAME_____<u>Joe Smith</u>_____

PURPOSE: To oversee Youth and Community serving projects. To evaluate current projects, as to their viability and to seek out new project ideas. Often the Chair of each service project serves on this Committee.

JOB DESCRIPTION:

To plan and review new project opportunities and new project chairs for future service projects, particularly those meeting the needs of children and youth.

To encourage Club participation in the major Programs and Activities.

EXPECTATION: To conduct one new, high visibility and high participation event during the coming year.

RESOURCES: Online assessment tool for community needs. Online planning guides and materials.

ACTION PLANS: As a Committee, create an action plan.

a) What is going to be done?
b) Who is going to do it?
c) When is it going to be completed?

This **ask** procedure solidifies the commitment and expectations between you the leader and the chairperson. This will make both of your jobs easier and more efficient as time goes by. Use this important tool as you do the next step, and **manage** their progress.

Manage Committee's Progress

Manage by first giving and reinforcing **ownership** to the Committee. Give them small credit for each positive step. Let them report their progress at Board Meetings and you compliment appropriately. Give them guidance and support but keep them accountable. Don't take ownership back. Be empathetic when they have difficulty; be enthusiastic when they have success. Take care not to fill in by doing everything yourself. Your job as CEO is to nurture and motivate others.

Recognize Committee upon Completion – and moderately recognize along the way

- Ongoing: Be optimistic, call them by name, listen with respect, show your appreciation
- Upon Completion: Be enthusiastic, give them recognition at Board, in E-newsletter and at meetings – invite applause. Give Chair a small token or memento of appreciation (and committee members if appropriate).

Using this format will make you more effective and save you time in the long run. This same general procedure is repeated many times with appropriate variations depending on progress. With time it will become semi-automatic. This is the job of President, "Asking (directive), managing (behaviors) and recognizing (outcomes)" achievement.

Note: Doing things that are not directly **driving actions to outcomes** are fine if you enjoy doing them and understand the implications.

Getting new members and inactive members involved

Light a fire under your members (motivate) and then run along beside them (manage) to the finish (recognize)! Light a fire by being enthusiastic, optimistic and friendly. Listen to them, respect them and call them by name. Recognize them by showing appreciation, sincerity, respect and friendship.

Use this same "ASK, MANAGE, RECOGNIZE" cycle to get new members involved or to bring members back into activation that have drifted away. Continue the same cycle with increasing accomplishments as people grow in activation and involvement.

To activate a new member or re-activate an inactive member:

ASK them to: Greet at the door, Pledge to Flag (or Toast), Recruit a new member, Arrange a program speaker, Lead the Pledge of Allegiance, Give an Invocation, Sell Raffle Tickets, Serve on a Committee, work on a project. For more involved: Be Chair of a Committee, Write Club Bulletin, Attend a Regional Conference with you.

ACT: Completion of task above

REWARD them: (Appropriate to the task difficulty) Write a personal note of "congratulations" or "thank you", Thank them in person, Pat them on the back, Smile at them, Shake their hand, Give the "thumbs-up", Recognize them from podium, Put their name in a newsletter, Put their name in Newspaper, Give them a "certificate", make them "Member of the Week", (ongoing) Recognize birthdays and anniversaries, give them an Award.

This is what a leader does, "manages his greatest assets – people" by motivating, nurturing and recognizing achievement. Repeating this basic cycle many times builds involvement, ownership, friendships. You are building an AWESOME T.E.A.M. !

Together Everyone Achieves More. You are molding your TEAM toward becoming a great organization!

12

GOAL SETTING - PROJECTING OUTCOMES OF MISSION AND VISION

Goal Setting is writing targeted "measurable outcomes" of a Mission Statement.

S.M.A.R.T. Goals should be Specific, Measurable, Achievable, Realistic and Time oriented.

Definitions we will use:

Purpose: (What) A specific, long-term statement of what defines the group.

Mission: (How) A statement of projected action(s) over the next few years – often followed by a Strategic Plan. **Goals** are projected outcomes of strategies and tactics.

Vision: (Why) A visual image emotionally describing an Outcome - expressed in speeches, branding tags, themes, logos and elevator speeches.

Goals are set in two ways:

- Goals set by the Leader – individually with unlimited time spent reflecting personal as well as organizational values
- Goals set by the Organization – in strategic planning session(s) usually with the board of directors and/or officers.

Ideally the leader would go through his goal setting followed by the organization going through their process as well. Goal-setting by the leader will be the focus now.

Note that ownership of these goals is important. Merging your goals with board or officer goals can be delicate, but if you get the respective ownership of each set of goals right, each set can be a powerful motivator.

Leader's goals start with the ultimate big picture purpose and mission. Ideally your goals will align with the organization or group you serve. How will you make your Community (or organization) better?

Now see if you can write an ultimate goal as president. If you're an optimist you might call it a "big audacious goal". Write what will be different this time next year. Who's lives will change and how?

> *Write an **ultimate goal** consistent with your Group's Mission. If it doesn't excite you try writing several others.*

Vision is visual image, painted by a leader and given to others. It inspires action toward a goal(s) with positive emotional motivation toward the mission.

Vision is one of a leader's most powerful tools. It will be repeated hundreds of times. Keep it varied, fresh and alive!

Start by writing expressions of your vision. If you are not comfortable with the power of vision, start by writing some ideas to each of the following.

Write your "Vision statement", "theme", or "branding line". (one short sentence)

Write/give an "elevator speech" of your Vision. (20 seconds)

Write/tell a "story" relating to what your Organization will do and how they will feel. (5 minutes)

Write some Goals:

Goals can be quite different from organization to organization and from group to group. Here is a menu of goals that may be pertinent to your organization. Write your own.

Members - your most valuable asset
How many new members will you personally recruit this year?
Will you lead by example?
How many members will your club add to its roster this year?
How many members will you lose?
What will be your club's "net gain" in membership this year?

Service, Outreach, Product
How many service projects will your club conduct?
What new and unique outreach program would you like to add?

How many widgets will you make and sell?

Will you expand to a new community or new product line?

Quality of Life – Personal benefits

Will your members be better people? Workers? Leaders?

Will your members enjoy their experience more? Happier? Self-confident

Will your members get to know each other better? Social goals?

How many of your members will get a promotion in the organization?

Write specifics as to how these goals will be measured.

Ownership of goals is an important motivating factor. Your overall goals can be shared in a speech on address to the organization. Committee goals should be assigned individually with the committee at the time when the committee appointments are made. Goals to other officers can be shared with them as a group ideally when selected.

Goals are a leadership tool. Goals drive behavior leading to outcomes.

Rewards, Awards and Recognition – Incentives to positive outcomes

As progress is made and small goals are met, reward recognition and appreciation are necessary to complete the cycle having an outcome of individuals leaving a feeling of success.

Recognition is short-term and given for progress or small accomplishments. It includes things like choosing a guest speaker to invite, giving an invocation, serving as a greeter at the door.

Awards are institutional recognition that is given for reaching large goals. The nature of the award is that the specific award is generally known when the leader accepts the goal. Awards may be available from a parent corporation or affiliate. It is wise for the leader to use these as incentives for both themselves and others.

Does your organization have access to any awards you would like to promote and present?

13

OUTCOME MANAGEMENT AND COMMUNICATION

The objective of management is to organize and track progress toward intended outcomes, both for you the leader and also for those you lead. It's kind of like your GPS (Global Position Satellite) of management. It's also your basis for when and what you communicate.

For you, the leader, simple systems like a calendar of "Asks" - things to do, is a good start. A chronological flow-chart of functions and due dates would be good as well. As complexity of positions, jobs, and tasks increase, more sophisticated management and communications systems have to be implemented.

Once organized, a data-base of overall action plans might serve as a good tracking/management tool. For example, consider the "committee appointment" process/form we recommend. At the end of each appointment, you asked the Chairperson to come up with an action plan listing "What, who and when". This is what you want to oversee, not to do it, and not to take back ownership, but to support and recognize progress.

Sample Management Spreadsheet

Name/Committee	What	Who	When	Comments
Smith/Activity	Select project	Sally	September 1	Making good progress
Smith/Activity	Get board approval	Sally	October 1	
Jones/Publicity	Invite publisher to meeting	Sam	November 1	Waiting for contact

If you have used a "Project Management" software in the past, that might be the best.

In conjunction with your data-base or flow-charts you need to communicate to keep contact and good relationships. Today we have so many options to communicate including email, texting, social media, phones and mail.

Use any and all communication options to keep in contact. But with so many messages everyday sometimes you can make a great impression going back to hand-written "note cards". Have addresses and a stack of note cards. Option – leave the inside blank for writing and put your organization's logo or branding tag on the front.

Send a Birthday Card when someone has a birthday.

Send a "Thank You" or "Congratulations" note whenever appropriate.

Use Phone to connect emotionally.

Email Newsletters are good weekly. Make them short with "links" to more information. Include: Time/date/location of next meeting, program speaker (reason to come), recognize those who participated in activity, announce coming events.

A good management tool to use in short management encounters is discussed in the One-Minute Manager by Ken Blanchard. It outlines a simple formula to praise, reprimand and set common goals in a very short time. This is an example of how you interact with others based on your knowledge of what they are doing (from your tracking systems).

These management tracking systems will keep you aware of where you are and what to do next as you work through repeated and variable cycles of influence. This directed persistence will gradually add up to great rewards and success.

14

CONDUCTING PRODUCTIVE MEETINGS

The success of meetings is measured in attendance. The most effective way to increase attendance is to give the attendee what they want at every meeting. That usually involves feeling appreciated, having fun, and getting or giving information that will make them a better person.

Secondary success comes from good promotions, programs with celebrity or featured speakers, meeting places that are easy to get to, meetings that are cost effective, offering attendees opportunities to meet other friends and fun. First impressions are important. When they walk into the meeting, are they greeted with a smile, warm welcome, hand-shake and program information?

In this section we will review these four types of meetings:

a. Strategic Planning
b. General Membership Meetings
c. Board Meetings
d. Committee Meetings

Meetings provide an opportunity to connect in person with a functioning unit of the organization. Every meeting has a specific purpose. A few pre-meeting preparations are essential for effective meetings that are productive and are respectful of people's time.

Before Each Meeting:

- Determine a purpose - What outcome do you expect for this meeting?
- Bring an Agenda and appropriate materials
- Look like a leader – Arrive early, have good attire and attitude, stand with shoulders back, head up, shake hands, smile with confidence. (This may seem silly, but it's also silly that people form impressions in ten seconds – it's reality)

Strategic Planning Meeting

At the beginning of a new administration it is a good idea to bring everyone into harmony with a common plan for the future. This can be helpful as ongoing issues arise. Actions then can be forward-looking rather than reactionary.

Sometimes strategic plans are made from scratch and sometimes they are modified from the year before.

What is a "Strategic Plan"?

It is a plan of actions for the next three to five years toward given outcomes. A strategic plan generally begins with the mission (or purposes) of the organization. From this three to five strategic thrusts are determined. Within each of these are several "objectives". And then a sub-group of objectives are tactics. Tactics are action plans listing, "What is to be done, Who is going to do it, and When?"

<u>What does a "Strategic Plan" look like?</u> (Basic outline to be expanded)

The strategic or long range plan begins with the mission of the organization and moves down in an outline reflecting the size of the issue. For example:

Mission: To provide positive programming
for our Community Teen Center

I. Strategic Thrust one (Member Growth)

    A. Objective one

        1. Tactic one

           a. Action Plans (What, Who and When)

I. Strategic Thrust two (Youth Activity)

    A. Objective one

        B. Objective two

II. Strategic Thrust three (Fund Raiser)

<u>Who attends a Strategic Planning (or Orientation) Meeting?</u>

Usually the members of the board or the officers (middle managers) or both attend. Of course, who attends depends on what is to be accomplished.

<u>Pre-preparation</u> **Orientation Meeting**

Send an email survey out one week in advance asking all attendees for opinions. Replies and names should be anonymous to get the most independent thought prior to meeting. The result then would be revealed to the attendees without any names on them as well. The meeting itself will have discussions including priority persuasions.

- What programs, activities or fundraisers should be dropped and why?
- What programs, activities or fundraisers should be added and why?

Sample Agenda for a <u>One-hour</u> Session – this should be called an <u>Orientation</u> Meeting.

ORIENTATION/PLANNING*: Presiding – President, Chair*
- *Welcome, introductions and **Purpose** of Meeting*
- *Review **Mission**, Organization (Incorporation, Bylaws, Policies), Parent Organizations, Financial Reports and Budget, Dues and Fees, Meeting times and locations, Rosters/Officers.*
- ***Status** Report: Membership, Assets, List ongoing Projects, Activities and Committees, Opportunities*
- ***STRATEGIC PLANNING****: Open discussion: what do we want to drop, what do we want to add? Projects, Activities, Fund Raisers, Promotions, Social Functions?*

Full-Day Retreat

A Full-day (or two half-day) session is an ideal way to really get into the process of planning. It could also be modified to fit a one half-day format. It is also done by the board and/or officers.

A board/officer retreat like this should have a facilitator. The facilitator should be experienced in leading planning sessions and be somewhat knowledgeable about the organization but independent of the politics and decision making.

The agenda is similar to the short one-hour meeting but with more meaning, depth and time to absorb and internalize ownership and commitment. A pre-meeting anonymous survey, designed by the facilitator, may be a good way to collect a large number of independent opinions – this is especially good for those who may be a little shy or less assertive than others at the meeting.

Sample Agenda for <u>One-Day "Strategic Planning"</u> retreat

Note that a good facilitator may have their own outline or system – use it.

STRATEGIC PLANNING RETREAT: *Formalities by President/Chair - Strategic Planning by a Facilitator*

– *Welcome, introductions and **Purpose** of Meeting*

– *Review **Mission**, Organization (Incorporation, Bylaws, Policies), Parent Organizations, Financial Reports and Budget, Dues and Fees, Meeting times and locations, Rosters/ Officers.*

– ***Status** Report: Membership, Assets, List ongoing Projects, Activities and Committees, Opportunities*

– **If this is a **Board**: Discuss form and function of Board, expectations and parliamentary procedures.*

– ***STRATEGIC PLANNING SESSION**: Open discussion will take a majority of the time. The format of the discussion will be provided by facilitator.*

  o *The format generally begins with a consideration of the Mission*

  o *Traditionally an Organization assessment tool is used such as S.W.O.T (Strengths, Weaknesses, Opportunities and Threats).*

  o *Then the Strategic Thrusts, Objectives, Tactics and Action Plans are created (or revised). See outline above.*

Sometimes, depending on the organization's size, finances, time and culture, a formal Strategic Planning Session is not conducted. Then the Chief Executive Officer goes through the planning process herself. Vision, mission and appropriate goals are still shared with the general membership.

General Membership Meetings - Having fun - being informed

General membership meetings are typically conducted with a meal and social in nature. They are for having fun, building relationships and sharing information. If business is to be conducted refer to the appropriate portions of the business meeting outline.

A good Club meeting is the result of careful planning and enthusiastic leadership.

Purpose: To have Fun, build relationships and provide information.

Bring an Agenda: If you have a lot of similar meetings consider making one basic agenda, leaving room under each item to write notes or add items. Photocopy 50 if you have weekly meetings. As you prepare each week, simply add names, announcements and notes. This is also a good agenda to FAX/email if the leader can't make a meeting.

As in our earlier discussion about giving a lot of small jobs (ask and reward) – just call them before the meeting with your requested ask (pledge, invocation, etc.) and put their name in the slot.

Sample agenda for General Member Meeting (Club)

General Member Meeting

Call to Order

Invocation_____ Pledge_____

Meal

Introduce guests

Recognize a "Member of the Month"_____

New Members Installations

"Joke of the Week"_____

Announcements

Introduce Speaker_____

Speaker's address_____

Announce next week's program_____

Draw for door prize/raffle/greeter prize_____

Adjourn

Fun, exciting meetings

As a general rule, if club meetings are **fun**, membership is active and growing. If you are a serious leader, you may want to put people on the agenda that can make people laugh.

Ideas for Having Fun:

- Joke of the week – ask for one volunteer per meeting, at the punch-line, members can vote with thumbs-up with laughter, or thumbs-down with moaning.
- Fun Awards like "Member of Week" for doing something noteworthy
    - Again pre-prepared light-hearted Certificates can be made in advance leaving room for the name to be printed on-site.

- Identify that Member: At beginning of the year, ask each member to submit a baby/infant picture. Make a large copy of each. Each week take one and have members guess who it is – win small prize.
- Smile contests – one-on-one, with a weekly elimination round.
- Birthday celebrations (singing)
- Sergeant at Arms: Collecting fines of small amounts of money for offenses has been common in the past. This is done in a fun way. Rewards for individual acts of heroism like getting your name in the local newspaper
- Each week a member gives a 2-minute talk about his/her hobby (or job)
- Fun Programs
    - Magician
    - Palm Reader
    - Masseuse
    - Games with Members

<u>Other Great Programs</u>:

- Invite Organization authorities to explain an area of Club function (Structure, Board duties, Activity overviews, fund raising ideas, etc)
- Invite local celebrities (TV, radio, historians.)
- Invite public officials (police, fire, librarians, etc.)
- Ask your Fellowship Committee for recommendations.

<u>Ways to build Relationships</u>

- Mystery "Secret Greeter": President asks someone to be greeter at the meeting but not tell anyone. Pick a number such as the 4th person to shake their hand and they would get a small prize when the secret greeter is revealed later in the meeting. (Or secretly identify best smile or handshake)
- Greeters at door helping with registration and nametags
- Social Events of all kinds

Publicly recognize members at meetings for their effort, achievement, and added value to the Club - Member of Week certificate

Business at Member Meetings

Generally the board of directors conducts the business of the organization. But occasionally general membership business is necessary. That would include an election of new officers and board members. This may also include matters of changing bylaws.

Care should be taken to conduct this business with all respect and guidance by the organizations bylaws and policies as well as parliamentary procedure. Review these before conducting business.

Board of Director Meetings

The Board of Directors conducts the business of the organization (other than those listed above as "Business at Member Meetings"). Board governance is specifically described in the organization bylaws. Read them carefully along with policies and parliamentary rules.

What is the Purpose of a Board of Directors? Generally, Boards oversee personnel issues including members and staff. Ideally the Board governs by a set of policies of "means and limits" – what the board wants done (means), and the guidelines/resources/limits under which it is to be completed. In addition to personnel a board oversees financial resources, projects, programs and promotions. A board is usually responsible for the organization's strategic plan.

What is the role of the President and Board Chairperson? The board chairperson presides, often setting the agenda. The chairperson speaks on behalf of the board generally representing only motions passed. If the president is also the chairperson, he plays two roles. Care is to be taken primarily to focus is on the board members getting fair input and participation; the gavel may be passed to another to preside if the chair wishes to enter the discussion.

If the President is not the chair, this allows him more freedom to focus on his agenda such as improving bylaws, finances and Policies to make the organization stronger.

Who are the members of the Board of Directors?

- Chairman of the Board: This person presides at the meetings of the Board. This position is sometimes combined with the office of President.
- President (if a different person): President is responsible for leading the Organization by carrying out Board directives as Chief Executive Officer.
- Secretary: Records the minutes of the Board Meetings. Secretary also does communication (correspondence, corporation reports, and legal documents). Only the motions are legally required since a Board only speaks through motions. Discussion summaries are often included depending on formality. Documentation of motions includes the name of the maker of motion and person seconding the motion, as well as the designation of pass or fail. Minutes become a permanent record of the club.
- Treasurer: Collects revenues (income) and disperses funds (pays bills) under constraints of a Budget. He keeps records of these transactions making them available to the Finance Chairperson and the Board Members.
- Vice Presidents: Back up the President with a wide variety of job descriptions.
- Directors at Large: Members elected by the General Members to represent them. It's generally helpful if they are Committee Chairpersons.

Sample Board Meeting Agenda:

Board Meeting Agenda – Chair presides over business

- *Call to order, Purpose of Meeting, Agenda corrections*
- *Motions/second with vote at any time*
- *Secretary Report (minutes available to members)*
- *Treasurer Report (finances available to members)*
- *Finance Committee should give an opinion of the accuracy*
- *Presidents or Executive Director Report, staff report*
- *Committee Reports and Recommendations (written option)*
- *New Business*
- *Adjourn*

Guidelines for Board adding and dropping programs: The two biggest priorities of whether to add or drop a program are the need of the community and having a qualified, dependable, committed chairperson.

The Board speaks only through motions. If anyone is speaking for the board they should support the position of the board on all issues passed.

Opinions are to be argued before the vote, not after. These votes should not be personal or prejudicial; they just are.

As a reality check, all things may not go as you hoped. Accept defeats from time to time but learn from them for the future. As a leader, choose your "battles" carefully. Don't expend time and energy of a small detail – think big picture, long term.

Be enthusiastic about the positives. Negative things can happen. This is a little exercise to consider, in advance. How might you handle some of these tough situations by keeping people's motivation high?

Dealing with management glitches: How you might handle these situations:

1. A committee chairperson who has an important project coming up next week does not show up to report to the board. What might you do as a president?
2. A committee chairperson is supposed to arrange an essay contest with local school officials. The entry deadline has passed. What might you do as president?
3. An email newsletter editor is highly motivated but is too "wordy" for emails and misses the essentials. How might you respond as a president?
4. A member brings a project to the board but they turn it down for whatever reason. How might you reach out to this person?

Committee Meetings

A Committee is a functional sub-group of an Organization with a specific task to complete. Committees do the work of the Board. They plan and implement. Committees may be:

- For a specific purpose (ad hoc) to organize and implement a project or activity.
- To meet a need that is ongoing (standing), such as marketing or recruitment.

Committee meetings are usually informal and don't require a formal parliamentary procedure so that planning and decision-making can move along appropriately. The creativity and organization skills of the chair are important to develop the project, plan for results, and follow through to a successful project.

The Committees report to the board of directors as they progress toward their goal.

Committee Size

- Each member of the board should serve on, or be chairperson of a committee. It creates more connectivity to what's going on.
- The size of a committee should be determined by the requirements of the assigned activity.
- Members may be appointed to more than one committee.

Committee Selection

- Look for a Chairperson who is enthusiastic about the cause of the committee. Successful experience in this area is helpful.
- "Interest" is perhaps the most basic qualification for serving on a committee. Other qualities for Committees could include time, commitment, special abilities, and dependability.
- Committees are one of the greatest training grounds for nurturing future leaders. Make that part of the committee's purpose.
- Note that background searches might be necessary for people working with children or money.

Preparation for Committees

When appointing a chairperson, use the format outlined under "Leading Your Team". That format gives clear description and expectations of the job the leader expects – and it is in writing. The information gained from this form should be shared with committee members.

The leader should empower the chairperson and the committee with a sense of ownership of their action plan. What things are to be done? When will they be done? Who will do each one?

Committee meetings may be two or three people meeting in a coffee shop or five to seven people around a table. The chairperson is responsible for moving the process forward steadily, with limited distraction, finishing with an action plan.

Sample Agenda for Committee Meeting

***Agenda for Committee Meeting** – by Chairperson*

- *Welcome and Introduce each other (or tell why each is interest in this committee)*
- *Define committee's objectives*
- *Spend a few minutes "brainstorming" thoughts about implementation (use a recorder or flip-chart)*
- *Now get formal writing an action plan (make a spreadsheet)*
- *What / When / Who / Comments*
- *Check work: do all endorse the concept? Do all have a role in implementation?*
- *Report progress and recommendations to the Board.*

The President (CEO) does need to know what is happening in committees he can achieve this by listening and supporting. The President does need to respect committee "ownership" of the project without micromanaging – this is leadership.

Meetings - Turning Negativism into Optimism

Attitude is a powerful catalyst for any organization. A positive attitude begins with the leader. The leader sets the tone for positive thinking, positive behavior and positive outcomes. Here are some techniques that can be used in a meeting situation:

Turning negativism to optimism

- *The Leader sets the tone by walking in the room positive, confident, smiling and shaking hands.*
- *Say, "Although we want to hear all opinions, we want to focus on the positives" in the stated purposes of the meeting*
- *When people make positive comments, give a gentle positive affirmation. Or compliment someone for being "positive"*
- *Do not put negative people to speak in your agenda*
- *Gumball jar for Optimism: Place a transparent jar in front of someone (head table more obvious). Each time someone speaks or acts in a "positive" manner put a gumball in the jar – each time someone speaks or acts in a negative manner take one out. See if you can fill the jar during the meeting.*
- *If someone is being really disruptive by being negative in a repetitive or non-productive manner, take them aside after the meeting to share what "negativism" is doing.*

15

SERVICE AND PRODUCT DELIVERY

This is where the "rubber meets the road." The service or the product that an organization delivers is the reason it exists. It is what sets the organization apart from the rest of the industry. This is what the leader is talking about when they share their vision with those on the front line of delivery.

Certainly the service or the product can be quite different from organization to organization. Therefore we will address this section in generalities. Consider these basic concepts for good service/product management:

Lead by Example

The purest form of leadership is to do the actions you want others to do. If you do it with fun, enthusiasm and vision, others will want to join in. Think of Tom Sawyer painting the white picket fence with so much fun, enthusiasm, and vision that he enticed his neighborhood friends to join in with him.

What ever it is your organization does, you do it. It is hard to ask someone to do something you haven't done.

Know your Service or Product

If it is service you deliver, know all of the programs, activities, resources and alliances the organization has to make an impact on others. If it is a product you deliver, know the technical components, raw materials, purchasing options and sales opportunities to make it the best for the customer.

Quality of Service or Product

A leader can build in systems (departments and committees) to focus on quality. Good oversight and management is what a leader can do for quality. Meetings with good quality education are helpful - including calendar dates and expectations.

Developing New Service or Product

Staying relevant in our changing world is necessary to attract people and customers. There are many ways to develop new services and products and bring them to market. As a leader consider the potential of those in your organization. Not only to they understand the organization but they have the idea and ability to implement. Your job is to create the opportunity to bring them forward, give them the resources they need to develop a new service or product while giving them the ownership and recognition they deserve.

Understand why people work to deliver your Service or make your Product.

Does a person work for the leader because they are paid or because they have a passion for making or delivering your product? Either way the leader must figure out why they work and how help keep them motivated – how to serve their needs.

And more important how are you able to impact the needs and wants of the customer or recipient of your service or product? Make this a part of your strategic plan.

Note that if you are not paying people, you have to really tap into their passions.

Using Vision to power the delivery

Vision, the image of the desired impact, can drive the people delivering the product and the recipients of the product. Vision feeds into marketing your business, both internally and outwardly. Use emotional stories, branding statement and visual themes to enhance motivation.

Finding and empowering key people

Your greatest asset is your people. Recruit the best people and give them the resources, training and incentives they need. Let them emerge to greatness.

Tactically, connect with your key people who can impact positive results. These key people are often a CEO type position such as a committee or project chairperson.

Find the right measurement tools that accurately assess what you deliver.

If you sell a product, sales revenues might be the easiest indicator to measure – it's certainly objective. Other measurement might include repeat sales and customer satisfaction.

If you give a service to meet a need, it is a little more difficult to find a good measurement tool. Consider using the following: Which is the best measure for your organization?

- Number of volunteers giving the services
- Overall funds donated or used to provide the services
- Time spent, and the quality of time spent giving service
- Number of recipients served

Grow the organization. Grow the product/service with your greatest resource – people.

16

SUCCESS THROUGH GROWTH

Growth of people delivering the product or service means success.

In a non-profit volunteer organization the services needed usually vastly exceed the organizations ability to meet those needs. Therefore the greatest impact on growth is to create more people-power or volunteers to deliver the needed services (product).

Growth = More Service = Success

This is a simple formula for success which works for about any service organization. Related outcomes to growth of members include:

- New Ideas, new energy
- More projects, activities and products
- Better programs
- More money
- More friends
- More resources for getting things done
- More new leaders – better chairpersons and officers
- Organization recognition and achievement
- Increased sense of pride and accomplishment

To be successful, any service organization needs to do both:

- Get new member (new clients)
- Keep current members (retain clients)

Service organizations are just like any business that needs new customers and repeat customers. The reason we list both needs is because they often involve a slightly different mid-set and therefore a slightly different strategy. For example getting a new member may incorporate an outgoing sales type of personality where keeping a member may be more of a "teaching type" person with orientation skills.

Increasing Organization Membership

Recruiting and keeping good members is essential for growth. Both recruiting members and giving them ownership and friendships is crucial for continuing solid growth. Following is a five-step cyclical process for getting and keeping good members.

How to increase Membership (Acronym P.R.I.M.A. for the best)

a. Participation – experiencing the joy of helping others

Cause drives participation. A member feels like they are making a difference in the lives of others. They are meeting a need greater than themselves. Participation is enhanced as friendships develop and interactions become meaningful on their own merit

b. Recruitment – Ask someone

All we have to do to get a new member is ASK. Of course, their odds of accepting our invitation increase if affiliation meets a need of theirs. Why would they join? New members join primarily for networking either for their business or for friendships. This makes a good friend a good candidate. Other good candidates are new people in the area who work in a people job.

A "no" is rarely rejection of you. It is "no" for now. Or it's "no" - it doesn't fit with my schedule. Try again sometime.

c. Induction, Orientation and Enrollment – give them ownership

Induct a new member with a formal ceremony. This is the best time to make a positive impression. It should inform both the new member with the cause to which they are joining; and it should inform the other members about who the new member is and what he does.

Orientation should be done at a separate time shortly after Induction. Orientation includes basic information about the organization's mission, fees, meetings and activities.

Enrollment is simply getting all the information on the new member relating to legal and contact information. At this time assess their interests and assign them as a member on a committee (or to a department). A membership application may include a section for the new member to express interests toward a specific committee in the list of committees.

Do you remember how you felt as a new member? The idea of this induction is to make them a real member – a shareholder.

d. Maintenance and Retention – keeping them

Do not delete anyone unless you visit them first, expressing why you would like them to continue with your organization. Listen carefully to what they say. Many issues are with cost versus benefits. Some issues relate to moving out of the area. Either way, thank them for their prior participation, and let them know they are always welcome in the future.

e. Attendance – make it a habit

At great member is one who participates in meetings and events by attending. Good club meetings that are fun, informative, and build relationships are basic to boost attendance. An email newsletter giving them a reason to come to the next meeting is good as well.

Incentives, games, drawings can make attending fun. Greeters and name tags help build relationships. Attendance then feeds back into participation.

How to perform a New Member Induction?

Schedule the induction date. Notify the new member and the sponsor. Bring materials - membership certificate or card and Information sheet. Also bring this (or other) installation guide with you.

Induction Ceremony *– Presiding: President or Membership Chair*

- *The President calls participants forward.*
- *The sponsor or membership chair introduces the inductee with a brief (2 minute) biography.*
- *The President invites the new member to repeat a pledge: "I solemnly promise to embrace the purposes and mission of this Organization (state name). I pledge to participate in the activities and programs of this Organization (state name)." (This should be written for your Organization)*
- *The President declares, "By the authority vested in me by the Board of Directors, I proclaim that you are a full member in the Organization (state name)."*
- *President could invite all members to welcome the new member with a round of applause as the President and others warmly shake the new member's hand.*

Brainstorm some of the unique ways you can make this a special event – to really make a positive impression on a new member.

This is an opportunity to make a lasting impression. Do it with respect and sincerity.

17

MARKETING, PROMOTIONS AND SOCIAL MEDIA

Meetings are the mainstay of experience, fun and friendships. Life-style experts say these are the mainstays of longevity and happiness.

But, our world is changing. Our relationships and outreach has expanded beyond face-to-face sessions, beyond geography, and beyond time frames. Cell phones, Internet, web-sites, email, texting, tweeting, Face Book new "apps" are opening up a dynamic and a novel potential. Virtual meetings have found a home in cyberspace as well.

Marketing, promotion and communication in general open up possibilities. If these aren't playing a major role in your organization now they will.

A basic marketing concept is that for every nine messages sent by an advertiser, three are heard; and it takes three times to hear a message before an action results.

Think of it. We live in a world where we are exposed to one to ten thousand messages a day by others competing for our time and attention. How can your organization compete with this?

Let's answer this in the context of a service organization. When I think of marketing, I think of delivering nine of the same messages in a variety of ways. Some I consider "high tech." Others, I feel, should be "high touch" – personal.

So what are your organization's communication strengths? Create a strategic marketing plan – strengths, weaknesses, opportunities and threats. You already have an organization mission/vision. In your plan under "mission/vision" would be a strategic thrust called marketing. State your objectives and create tactics and action plans.

When developing market plans, start with your vision. How can life be different if you join our organization or use our service? Market those benefits.

If you are local and have a connection with the community, this could be the access to your marketing. If funds are limited and commitment is high, you have low-cost, high impact options such as:

- Community visibility at events, activities and fund raisers
- Local newspapers often are looking for interesting community initiatives and photos.
- Using special programs of interest at meetings could also attract outside people as well as press. Fliers in public places around the community can both inform of these programs while the flier itself draws attentions.
- Does your parent organization have materials and guides for marketing? Use them.

18

INTERNATIONAL LEADERSHIP

Seek first to understand – then to be understood.
– Inspired by the Prayer of Saint Francis

One of my life's greatest insights was learned through many years of eye care missions, living with and sharing thoughts with a diversity of culture. People all over the world have hopes and dreams – understanding these form the basis of connecting organizations around the world.

This Chapter will focus on Volunteer International Non-Governmental Organizations. These typically have affiliate local or state chapters with local volunteers providing most of the outreach services.

Large international organizations can be quite complex and multifaceted. It is important to understand the design and structure of how the various parts work together.

Rather than discuss all leadership methods, I have limited discussion to a number of strategies and tactics that have produced big results for myself. The important thing to understand is the thought process that makes up the strategy and how it is used in leading to greater results. Keep in mind that these strategies may not fit other leaders that have other strengths or other organizations with different operations.

Successful leadership strategies will be discussed with an emphasis at the top of the organization – President or Chief Executive Officer.

Leading is delegating; and as the top leader, almost everything you do has to do with delegating. The strategies follow the same "ask, act, reward process" as used at any other level of leadership. People are the key to success – yours, theirs and the organization's success. Many people and many actions will be revolving around you at once. A good perspective and sense of priorities is helpful to navigate through things that are paying big dividends and things that are not. A top leader has to have the future planned and be able to respond quickly and appropriately as new issues arise. With good leadership perspective and persistence you can drive actions to outcomes.

Confidence Grows from Experience

Much of what is discussed in this international chapter assumes that you have already acquired substantial leadership skills to leading at this level. This discussion is only meant to build upon a foundation of leadership you already have. These early leadership experiences and successes have given you the confidence to meet other leadership challenges.

CREATING NEW ORGANIZATIONS

In 1985 I learned how to build new Optimist chapters in nearby communities accompanied by my mentor. This became my introduction in building new organizations from the ground up.

By starting these new organizations I experienced the process and learned the basics of structure, membership and purpose that represent a cause. It became an opportunity to try creating a new organization that meets international eye care needs from the ground up.

Having had the experience of being a local president of a service organization, I was ready to start my first new organization whose purpose would be to lead eye care delivery missions to other countries. This new organization would consist of Michigan optometrists, ophthalmologists and opticians who were willing to donate their time at their expense to bring their talents to helping others across the world see.

This, of course, was a giant leap in leadership, but, I had a purpose and I had confidence. What else did I need? That was really all I needed to start; with a good plan and a lot of work and committed people joining the cause, we made it happened.

We initiated an affiliation with Voluntary Optometric Services to Humanity – (VOSH) which gave us a resource for building a chapter in Michigan. Much time was spent over the next year just talking to people and discovering interest. Building a new organization involved a one-on-one contact until you connect with a similar passion in one or two others. This is the tipping point to success. When key people embrace a purpose and take ownership, you've got a movement.

VOSH-Michigan was officially formed in 1986. I served as president for the first three years. At the beginning Dr. Nelson Edwards was one of those key people who became greatly involved. We went through all the steps of incorporation, setting bylaws, creating budgets and information pamphlets to help spread the word. The momentum began to build.

Awesome Top Strategy for building new mission sites

Our greatest organizational growth strategy that allowed us to expand around the world was initiated by Dr. Nelson Edwards.

He would lead an International Eye-Care Mission from the very beginning by finding a location, sponsor and host, recruiting the eye-care professionals, arranging the travel, and securing health care permits.

While on the mission he would spend the seven to ten days working with the other doctors to not only teach but to find one doctor that would take over the trip for the next year and beyond.

He repeated this strategy almost every year for about ten years. Finding a leader to sustain the trip worked about sixty percent of the time which made our steady, solid, sustainable growth possible.

VOSH (Voluntary Optometric Services to Humanity) – Michigan grew steadily. Eventually we were drawing the best professionals in the state and conducting productive eye care mission trips each year to six to seven different countries.

Creating a new organization from the very beginning is an exciting experience. You have the freedom and ownership to make it yours – multiplying the good you can do for others.

Resources: "High Touch – High Tech"

A good guideline to model resources is though an appropriate use of "High Touch – High Tech". These are issues of form matching function.

Technology is the most efficient way to disseminate and organize large amounts of information.

Administratively a large international organization is probably best suited to providing online information and easy access to financial and enrollment operations.

But a system that personally connects with people can lead with emotion. People know people and officers do understand what their people want, need and fear.

Emotion is the reason a volunteer acts. Information gives the volunteer the base from which to act.

Websites are a basic. Navigation within and access to the website is a challenge. It is ideal to combine a knowledgeable cyber expert with a volunteer who can identify with all the levels within the organization to truly create a user-friendly powerful web resource. This is easy to say, but not easy to do. Finding a good design that is cost effective and can empower an officer or committee chairperson gives your organization an incredible competitive advantage.

"High touch" is the personal part of leadership that connects with people's emotional needs. The reality is that most people act out of emotion. Their passions are what drive them to greatness; and their passions are what drive them to seek information from the internet.

As a top leader, think analytically about "form and function" and emotionally on "vision and motivation." Consider the costs and benefits of every meeting, and every committee, and everything else you use.

High Tech Resources:

- Websites, social media
- Electronic transfer of dues, fees, contributions and finances

- Easy access to communication with a large variety of target officers, committee, groups.
- Quick responses to organizational or humanitarian needs
- Expert information given from "call-in" locations
- Online meetings, forums and project management
- Ability to reach out globally

High Touch Resources:

- Mentorships
- Help officers succeed by empathizing, supporting, cheerleading, problem solving, improving attitude and molding behavior.
- Be a catalyst to connecting people to internet resources
- Organizational education at club meeting programs (20-minute topics: self-improvement, board administration, project and activity orientation, etc.
- Specific purpose face-to-face seminars and symposiums
- Strong local influence

This is only an overview of providing resources. It takes work to create and give great content with easy access.

Part of a leader's role is to help others succeed. Providing good, user friendly planning guides, financial tools and information is part of motivations – removing barriers to success – making success accessible.

Mentoring C.E.O.'s – Presidents of Junior Optimist Octagon International

Because of the complexities and diversities of international organizations, mentoring is probably one of the best ways to work with a new Chief Executive Officer.

Generally this initial phase is spent connecting their experience and perceptions to their new job descriptions and expectations. This is generally loosely structured conversation listening to what inwardly motivates them; what are their wants, needs and fears. This forms a basis for productive consul and exchange of ideas on a wide variety of subjects.

After spending two years as the C.E.O. (President) of Voluntary Optometric Services to Humanity – International I turned to mentoring young Junior Optimist Octagon International Presidents. JOOI is a 16,000 member youth organization in North America.

One of my greatest joys in mentoring five young international Presidents of JOOI is to see these young people take on new and challenging jobs in leadership and grow exponentially from the experience – even in the course of a year! Most of their personal growth was internally generated. My instruction and guidance was often minimal. Just being nearby and available helped the mentoring process.

The Power of a C.E.O.

The reality is that a Chief Executive Officer or President has much greater power and opportunity than anyone in the organization. That is simply because he has control over everything in the organization (within legal bounds). The C.E.O. can utilize structure and resources to implement incredible strategies for positive change and success.

Preparing a CEO to take office gives them credibility of competence and visibility in leading by example.

Growth toward Success

In a volunteer organization growth is a good measure of success. Member growth is meaningful because it equates best with service outreach. Success could be measured by the number of recipients or beneficiaries of the services. It could also be measured by the monetary value of its services or just total revenues/expenditures. It is good to measure all but decide on the best measure that fits your organization – this is the outcome by which you are measuring your success and the success of your organization.

Measure what you manage. Philosophically it would be nice if we could measure the emotional changes, impact on lives, and lives saved from our organization's services. As you know that is not possible, but it is possible to keep an emotional vision at the forefront of motivation. Therein lies a dilemma, you "sell with emotion" but "manage with measure". Getting those two right, makes you a Leader.

Change the Clubs – Change the Organization

We must change clubs to change the organization! Clubs are likely the functional unit of your organization. Clubs and members provide the service – your product. Leaders, administrations and organizations can only succeed if the delivery unit (club) succeeds. Service businesses exist to keep their clients (clubs) and get new clients (clubs).

The "key" that unlocks change in a club is the C.E.O. Make every President at least a better C.E.O. and encourage some Presidents become great C.E.O.s.

Think percentages - Multi-faceted - Global Strategies

Do not think of leadership methods producing "all bad" results or "all good" results. Instead think percentages when dealing with large numbers. For example if seven percent of one hundred thousand of your members currently recruit all of the new members, think "what can be achieved if recruiters are increased to ten percent"? That one sub-strategy can make a huge annual improvement in member strength.

Put together a few of these strategies and great success can be achieved.

Think Molding and Nudging Change

The mindset of an international leader is not instant change and groundbreaking turnarounds. It is about change by gently nudging, or redirecting, or molding behavior and actions. With global approaches you can touch one person at a time but that may mean to neglect others. As discussed earlier, change is gradual and implemented after many repeated cycles.

Getting the Best Committee Chairmen/Members

If you have a hundred committee members to appoint in a large International Organization, it is almost impossible to do from your personal memory of impression. It is also not fair to their talents and passions to pass over people because you do not know of them. This is why it is imperative of seek out the best:

- Those best qualified, experienced with proven performance records
- Those with the passion and interest in working in a specific area

To do a good job usually takes much hard work seeking out recommendations and reviewing data-bases. It is also important to call people you know who have worked with candidates to learn more about your prospects. And finally while making the appointment with the individual keep an open mind even if it takes changing them to another appointment on another committee.

Admittedly this takes concentration, time and a personal connection. These highly committed people will be much more likely to excel. You will then manage each of their efforts with your "management metrics and communication" system.

The appointment or search aspect of finding new leaders, on its own, begins a relationship process.

Relationship Building with new Officers and Appointees

Being international, first contact should be as personal as possible – phone and/or note cards. The basics are early contact for "congratulations" soon after the election or appointment. And a welcome might begin with talking about them and their families. It's also good to talk about anything that would help establish a relationship. The first phone call might also be about sharing contact information, calendar dates and such.

This is followed by basic information of job description and expectations. In large organization there is usually a formal process for setting up new officers and appointees which gives the leader more freedom to develop the relationship first.

Relationship building is not only important for working relationships, but it often becomes the beginning of deep, lasting friendships.

Relationship building is very personal and quite diverse in the way that it is expressed. As a frame of reference, consider that relationship building is ongoing and interwoven into the fabric of leadership and service. Therefore we are going to continue relationship building as an ongoing integral part of leadership.

The ultimate benefit of relationship-building is to understand what that new officer/appointee wants or needs from the job ahead.

The operant process of leadership is to make both of your dreams come true.

PREPARING LEADERS for SUCCESS

Start Preparing Officers and Appointees Immediately!

Meet with them soon after they are elected or appointed if possible. It is much more effective to develop ideas in a new leader than to change ideas that are already established. The purpose of the initial meeting is primarily to begin building a relationship but also to inform them with calendar dates, job description and expectations.

Arranging this meeting may take imaginations since officers in an international organization are widely dispersed. Each situation and access is different. Plan a way that you can make early contact and a significant impact. This is a top strategy for success.

Plan to develop C.E.O.'s (state governors)

State governors in many organizations play a role of chief executive officer. Often state governors are CEO's half-way between the international CEO and the local CEO. As such careful and extensive preparation is needed.

Preparing Local Presidents and Officers

If you have thousands of these officers you can't do it yourself. Teach state leaders to use parallel teaching techniques that were present in their conferences - assist Governors to prepare Presidents. Here are a few tactics you might consider:

Tactics to prepare many local Officers

- *Send materials (calendars, contact information, leadership tips) about their office in advance. Do not overload them with a large volume. Use basic information directed at only what they need immediately. Keep in mind people have different ways of learning – take preparation to them.*
- *Teach and show your state leaders how to prepare their local officers in a similar manner that they have been trained. Give them curriculum, handouts, PowerPoints and guides.*
- *Online, remote preparation and management can be a great tool as well. Get officers connected with contact information, emails, website orientation, etc.*

MANAGEMENT METRICS and COMMUNICATION

In preparation for a job as President, use the data-bases for appointments. Spend some time creating an effective tracking system showing what people are doing. Your primary job is to ask – act – reward. This system will give you the base information.

Performance information can be used in all phases of managing the organization – primarily officers and committees. The information is used for making phone calls categorized by time zones. It is also packaged for newsletters, monthly website updates and emails individually designed for targeting each component of service. It is also great for creating charts and graphs used in management meetings.

Tracking Measurable Outcomes

For each state or regional leader you could track:

- Member adds (recruitment)
- Member deletes (losses)
- New clubs/chapters built
- Dues delinquent
- Add a column for comments

Every organization is different but management tracking systems can keep the leader knowledgeable about the performance of many other leaders while respecting chains of command.

Consider emphasizing calls that are focused on positive actions. Let them know you are going to make them accountable. Ask leading questions so you can spend a lot of listening. If they are working hard, telling you all about it is a highly motivational.

International Presidents options for reaching members directly

The International President, using his time wisely, has several potential strategies to directly impact club presidents:

- Targeted phone calls: Call volunteers that are building new clubs/chapters - in progress and upon completion.
- Call top recruiters of new members. Call organizers of successful programs.
- Outreach Bus/RV Tour: This can be an effective, high-profile way to reach out to volunteers who are delivering the service. This takes careful planning to hit the highest profile events, including newly formed clubs.

- Conferences: Visits to state conferences can be productive if you have good attendance. Area-wide conferences may be more effective in that you can connect with more leaders.
    - o Note: When an international representative is visiting a conference their performance metric is "what happens in the three months following their visit."
- An international convention is a great opportunity for the International President to connect directly with officers and members. Conventions are planned to include many of the organization's sub-groups with task oriented meetings/receptions. The President should be aware of each meeting and attend each with a pre-determined objective in mind – and a short targeted message.

Reaching Members in print

The international magazine is perhaps the best way to connect with every member. It puts something in front of them that they can see. The editorials can be inspiring and initiate action. Think about the front cover of the magazine. What is it you want everyone to do? Or know?

A website is another good place to connect with members. Video clips can be powerful not only to connect with the president but to learn and be inspired. These systems need easy access to drive people to the website. This can be done by the magazine, email, newsletter, or a recommendation by a friend or club president.

Rewards, Awards and Recognition

Rewards are many and include the great feelings we get by doing a good job and making a positive difference. Awards are institutional recognitions – annual and anticipated. A great deal of informal recognition utilizing a wide variety of creativity and enthusiasm is a must – it is part of the "pay" a leader can give volunteers.

When considering international awards, consider formal awards that are consistent with the desired outcomes of the organization. They should be cost effective, easy to verify, and expedient to present. The awards should be promoted and held in high esteem.

Building New Chapters

Thousands of things happen every year with hard working dedicated people. In your organization consider the greatest thing anyone can do. Make these people heroes in your organization like building a new chapter.

Building new chapters (clubs) is the strategy five times more likely to bring growth than any other! A new chapter also brings five times the people-power to deliver services.

19

THE FUTURE OF VOLUNTEER ORGANIZATIONS

A leader's mandate long-term is to foretell the future and to change the future for the benefit of mankind. Earlier in this book we discussed the theory of the nature of things to grow, mature and influence. We did not discuss how things lose influence and decline.

Successful growth paradigms that sustain organizations come and go. Very few are enduring forever. The "Civic Service Model" of volunteerism was born in the early 1900's as was the internal combustion engine. Both are functioning successfully and if kept well-tuned, can continue successfully. But they are not the future of volunteerism.

Our world is changing and we must change to be a growing, thriving force for a better future. For thousands of years volunteerism has been a personal mater among friends or relatives with needs. This will continue. Because of the size and systemic nature of needs today, only organization can overcome barriers of financing and barriers of geography.

Since the early twentieth century government has taken a more active role in meeting people's needs. This is working quite well with financing that could not be achieved with typical volunteer involvement. Foundations have become viable components of meeting needs over a similar time period. Currently governments provide the tax incentives to each although support is beginning to peak and wane. The emerging model over the last few decades has been the growth of private for-profit corporations using combinations of charitable and promotion accounts to partner with volunteers on specific causes or short term events of public service.

Currently the greatest growth of volunteers and fundraising is coming from the internet and electronic communication. If ranked purely by dollars or participants, these organizations are clearly leading the way. Note that the "personal touch and impact on lives" may not be such a significant outcome.

As we lead our organizations into the future, it behooves us to think strategically, think creatively, and invest in change that empowers us to <u>Lead by Driving Actions to Outcomes</u>.

POSTLOGUE

I was a rather normal person until I met my mentor. Phil's iceberg analogy gave me confidence. Charisma and motivational speaking were not strengths but my strategic planning, implementing and empowering people were strengths that were powerful but not readily visible. This understanding that most of leadership is unseen (below the surface) turned to an advantage because it let me put others in the spotlight.

By using this basic process of leading with <u>ask – act - reward</u> repetitive cycles, your dreams and aspirations can come true. Remember, people do what makes sense to them. It's simple – it's about them, not you.

As future officers and leaders yourselves, my hope is that this book on leadership will give you confidence and abilities that you can learn. Embrace this process as your own realizing the tactics may change but the principles are eternal.

This process works. Although not all my initiatives have worked, all C.E.O. offices have produced significant growth with benefits to many people.

I'm blessed with so many great friends from my V.O.S.H and Optimist experiences. There were times when I was down, but my friends bolstered me. Some of my greatest rewards are seeing people

I've worked with do well – and seeing kids I've worked with succeed in life.

> *The Orchestra Leader didn't write the music.*
> *Nor did he make a sound.*
> *The talent of each musician is uniquely artful.*
> *Each instrument sings its own melodious tone.*
> *Why is this symphony so enchanting to my soul?*
>
> *- An Orchestra Leader*

The ultimate outcome of using the theory, cycles of influence, strategies, performance metrics and motivation is making a better world. Your efforts result in the smile on the face of a child who has just given her first speech, the look of wonder in the eyes of someone who is seeing for the first time, the exuberating breaths of kicking your first soccer goal and a thousand other small things that enhance people's lives.

That is your mission as a leader. Your Success impacts the lives of people.

INDEX

BIBLIOGRAPHY

These books were influential in the writing of this Book.

Blanchard, Ken, <u>The One Minute Manager</u>

Bergson, Henri, <u>Creative Evolution</u>

Carnegie, Dale, <u>How to Win Friends and Influence People,</u> 1936

Duhigg, Charles, <u>The Power of Habit, Random House: Why we do what we do in Life and Business,</u> Random House, 2014

Fulgrum, <u>I Learned Everything I Need to Know in Kindergarten</u>

Robert Heller, <u>Motivating People</u>, DK Publishing, New York, 1998

Listenberger, Michel, <u>Self-Utility: A Theory of Everything,</u> Author House, Bloomington, Indiana, 2009.

McNally, David, <u>Even Eagles Need a Push</u>, Dell Publishing, New York, 1990

Maxwell, John, "<u>21 Irrefutable Qualities of Leadership</u>", Maxwell Motivation Inc., Georgia, 1998

Reicher, Stephen D., Haslam, S. Alexander and Platow, Michael J., "The New Psychology of Leadership" Scientific American Mind, August/September 2007.

Swimme, Brian, "The Universe is a Green Dragon", Bear and Company, Rochester, Vermont, 2001

Walsh, Jack, <u>Winning</u>,

ABOUT THIS BOOK

<u>Lead by Driving Actions to Outcomes</u> simplifies the process, brings focus and amplifies results. Learn and use the axiom <u>Ask – Act - Reward</u> to change yourself, others, and organizations. Success is yours as you lead local volunteers in making a better community. With practice, leading becomes a habit as large organizations flourish in making a positive impact on the lives of many.

Sharing this process with others can leverage your success as well as build lasting friendships.

Whatever your leadership purpose is, this book can help you take a giant step toward making it reality.

BIOGRAPHY: MICHEL LISTENBERGER, OD, FVI

Dr. Listenberger has an extraordinary record of service and performance leading volunteer service organizations over the last thirty years. He has led as the President, CEO and Chairman of the Board for two International Non-Government Organizations. Under his leadership Optimist International (4th largest civic service organization in the world) produced the most growth in twenty years as well as increased total value of services to over one billion dollars. Serving as International President and CEO of Voluntary Optometric Service to Humanity (largest professional free eye care delivery organization in the world) he oversaw missions in twenty-five emerging nations.

Not only has he been successful in his own right, he has taught other international C.E.O.'s. Being chairman and advisor of a 16,000 member youth organization (JOOI) he mentored five International Presidents and boards.

His education includes a Bachelor of Science and Doctorate of Optometry from Indiana University and a Certificate of Creative Management from the University of Notre Dame. Dr. Listenberger founded Niles Vision Clinic which has grown to a successful three-doctor clinic.